On a
GALLOWAY ISLAND

Fulfilment of dreams and a spiritual journey

The fulfilment of dreams and a spiritual journey

Revd. Beryl M Scott

ON A GALLOWAY ISLAND

CONTENTS

FOREWORD - September 2003

This week my daughter came up to Galloway for a short break. We walked along the track from Rockcliffe to Castle Point, and scrambled down the steep bank to the beautiful, sandy bay enclosed by cliffs and rocks. Three men were waist deep in the sea, the tide had turned and they were busy baiting their fishing lines, hoping for a good catch on the next tide. The Solway Firth was rough, waves were dashing against them, soaking them and making their balance precarious, yet they were obviously enjoying pitting their strength against the sea. My thoughts were transported back forty five years to the time when John and I revelled in the exhilaration of battling against the sea and the weather; struggling through the water up to our waists as we raced against time before the tide covered the rack leading to the safety of our island home. We had many adventures, experienced wonderful times, saw natures spectacular beauty, encountered great hardships, yet it was the best time of my life, a time of opening doors and looking to the future. We had no modern amenities, little money, but great hopes and dreams for the future. Life has come full circle and I have returned to Galloway and it is good walking in the places where so much happened, reliving such vivid memories, renewing friendships and giving thanks for a full life. It is time for me to share some of the adventures, excitement, beauty, hope and blessings in the following story, which I started to write on the first day of the millennium, and finished unaware that shortly the opportunity would present itself for my return to bonny Galloway.

INTRODUCTION

The beginning of a new millennium is exciting, perhaps a time to look forward to future adventures, and certainly a time to wonder about what life may hold in store for us. I do much of my day dreaming of the future, for myself and my family, as I walk each morning on Cannock Chase or Gentleshaw Common. This is a special time for me, when I can enjoy the beauty of God's universe, whatever the weather. It is also a spiritual time as I enjoy the solitude, only meeting the occasional person up early to walk their dog. That first morning of the new millennium was no exception, and I set out while it was still dark to enjoy the peace and quiet of the Common. I met no one that morning, every one was tucked up in their beds after the festivities of the night. The voices of revellers and the swishing and banging of the fireworks had continued well into the morning. As I walked towards the common the darkness began to lighten, and I was looking forward to witnessing a magnificent dawn and sunrise on the first day of this unique year, the heralding of a new millennium. It was disappointing, there were no brilliant bands of tangerine, or golden glow on the horizon, the eastern sky was grey and dull. Yet the sky above was clear with a crescent moon shining, and a brilliant planet visible as the dawn emerged. The thin mist below prevented any hope of a spectacular sunrise. In fact, the mist was getting thicker and soon the moon too disappeared and everywhere was shrouded and mysterious.

My disappointment was short lived. As I left behind the silent, lonely moor and walked along the lanes, I was greeted by a mini dawn chorus. A robin was singing heartily, greeting the new millennium, starlings were lined up on a roof busily chattering away, rooks cawed as they flew overhead. I could hear the cooing of pigeons, and the raucous cries of magpies, the call of a blackbird and the twittering of sparrows. It was a magical moment, and more than made up for the absence of the sunrise. The early morning with its mystic, shrouded beauty made me ponder on the veiled future. We often wish that we could see into the future, and know whether our dreams and longings will be fulfilled.

Fifty years ago I had many dreams and longings, and at that time would not have believed that most of them would be fulfilled. Only a few years later I was experiencing the exhilaration of a new life filled with the unexpected. No longer were my surroundings those of a built up city, still looking drab from the war years, with food rationed and houses difficult to come by. A new beginning on a small island turned my prosaic life of daily routine upside down, bringing undreamed of challenges, life that was ruled by tide and weather. There would be challenges of sea and gales bringing excitement and danger, yet untold beauty with new experiences unfolding. The life would be primitive, without mains water, gas or electricity, with no neighbours from whom help could be sought in times of need. It was to be a life enjoyed to the full, the fulfilment of dreams and a widening of my understanding of the world and nature. Above all it would be a renewing and deepening of my spiritual life, and a change of direction in my spiritual journey. Dreaming and planning can bring satisfaction and joy, even if our fantasies are never realised, but it is a bonus when the dreams become reality and are far more adventurous than in our imagination.

CHAPTER 1 **The Beginnings**

"And now faith, HOPE, and love abide, these three; and the greatest of these is love" (1Corinthians ch. 13 v 13.)

My reflections, on that misty, strange, millennium morning, have carried me back over time as I remember my journey through life, both the physical journey and the spiritual journey. As I pondered on those early years, I recalled all my hopes and dreams for the future, and realised that many of them had been fulfilled. The time scale was not of my making, for when we are young we are eager and impatient, thinking that we know what is best for us and wanting everything to happen quickly.

My parents were not church members, yet they took me for baptism, and I am very grateful to them for they tried to keep the vows they had promised on my behalf. I am saddened when clergy turn parents away who seek baptism for their children, because they are not regular attenders at Church. Perhaps, the parents are not really aware of the true significance of baptism, but if they are instructed and want to continue with the sacrament, then who are we to judge that they are not sincere and will not fulfil their vows. My parents did not go to church, but taught me to pray and sent me to Sunday School at the age of three, and there I heard the wonderful stories from the Bible about Jesus. I became a Christian at a very early age and grew up as a follower of Jesus. My parents were happy for me, although I remember an aunt expressing her disapproval, and warning mother that I was developing religious mania. Although baptised in the Church of England, the only Sunday School in the new housing area where we lived was held in the local school, and later I realised that it belonged to a group of Christians called Brethren.

When I was fifteen I met my first boy friend whose longings and visions of the future were similar to mine. We met through church and our friendship grew. We had much in common, we both hoped that our lives would be spent serving God and the community. Perhaps, we would become missionaries, or serve the church in some other full time capacity. Our childhood was spent in city surroundings, and one of our dreams was to live in the country, even on a small island, although the chances of this were slim. We were only sixteen when we made promises to each other that we would marry. People often wondered why we were never officially engaged, with a ring and a party. Our secret promises to each other were the only engagement we needed. The hopes for our married life included, serving God full time, having two children, living in the country, and one day moving to Scotland. Life on an island was only a dream, and too much to hope for. We were both still at school, so all these reflections were for the future.

John loved music and introduced me to good music, for my musical education had been sadly lacking. His great love and hobby were pipe organs. We were involved in the usual Sunday services, teaching in the Sunday School and attending prayer and Bible study evenings. On Saturdays we often set out on our bicycles into the country, usually ending up at a church where John asked permission to play the pipe organ. He had taught himself to play, and had read every book that he could find about pipe organs. The librarian, on one occasion, suggested that he wrote a book about organs himself, since he had exhausted their records. In those early days, very few organs were powered by electric blowers, and I usually ended up pumping the bellows by hand. During church services a choir boy was often used to pump the organ, and woe betide him if he did not keep the bellows inflated during a loud hymn, when all the stops were drawn. John would have liked to join a pipe organ firm when he left school, but the only way he could do this was by becoming an apprentice at the age of fifteen. His parents wanted him to use his education and brains in, what they considered, a more fulfilling occupation.

We both left school at eighteen, forgoing university. This seemed the right thing to do so that we could earn some money in preparation for setting up home, and also repay our parents a little for allowing us to stay on at school. We lived on the outskirts of the city and John worked in research and continued his education in production and mechanical engineering by taking evening classes and day release from his firm. After I left school I worked in a chemical laboratory at the Imperial Chemical Industry. The huge plant produced copper sheets and pipes, and it was essential that the correct percentage of copper, along with other elements, was used to give the products the right strength and properties. Samples from the mill were analysed regularly to ensure that the strength and malleability of the metal were maintained. I also analysed a number of other products. The firm produced cartridges so the cartridge paper and the gunpowder were analysed. On one occasion I had the temperature of the oven too high when drying out the sample, and a mighty bang caused quite a diversion when the oven blew up. Pollution was not monitored as much then as it is now, but we did test the effluent present in the river, which flowed through the works. One duty caused great suspicion amongst the canteen staff; about once a month we took samples of the food to determine the vitamin content. On one occasion a stray kitten came into the lab, and its loud mews pointed to its hunger. We mixed the dehydrated food from the last testing with water, and the hungry cat ate it with relish. The meal had been fish and chips! In the laboratories were many young men who had served in the airforce, and they were high spirited and used very colourful language. It was difficult to witness to my beliefs as a Christian, but people respected me for it, and when I was around, they moderated their language.

Stories of country life were read avidly, together with exciting stories of life on an island. These fired our imagination and gave us a determination that one day we would experience such adventures. John had traced his family tree to Scotland and he wished very much to visit Scotland and perhaps live there. These were all dreams for the future, but one dream did come true. After waiting seven years we had at last saved up enough money to get married and set up home together. This wasn't easy for in the early nineteen fifties even finding a house was almost impossible. New houses were being built, but only people with children stood any chance of buying one. We thought of buying an old boat and living on that, or even a bus to convert into a travelling house, but the practicalities of these ideas made us abandon them. We did eventually find a house, in the town of Sutton Coldfield. It was a two bed-roomed terraced house, with no bathroom and an outside lavatory. John's mother had queued for long periods, while we were at work, before eventually succeeding in finding us this home. It cost £1050, an unbelievable price in this day and age, but a lot of money at that time. For seven years we had saved hard, spending as little as possible, often walking long distances to save the bus fare, but even so a large mortgage was still necessary. The house was small, and in the middle of a row of old houses. The paint work was dark brown and it was rather gloomy. We furnished it mainly with second-hand furniture, unlike the first homes of many couples today in this age of buy now and pay later. It was our first home together and we were very happy. There was no daily shower in those days. We kept a galvanised bath hanging on the kitchen wall and this was brought down and filled with water, heated from a coal fired boiler used for washing clothes and heating large quantities of water. The toilet was built onto the house next to a coal shed, and both were entered from outside the house. The small back garden was easily managed, and as we had no hand shears, I cut the wee front lawn with a large pair of scissors!

Some memories of the first year of married life stand out. Behind the row of terraced houses was an embankment and trains laboured up the slope of the track. One night we were rudely awakened from sleep by a huge bang. We leaped out of bed expecting to see a crashed train rolling down the embankment. As we struggled into some clothes, we were met by a cloud of dust. The ceiling of the second bedroom had fallen down and the whole house was smothered in particles of rotten plaster. Another incident remains clear. We loved water, and often picnicked in Sutton Park, sitting by a stream in a lovely meadow. Our new house had water bubbling up in the middle of the garden. We thought that, may be, this was a natural spring, and we planned to make a water feature in the garden. Unfortunately, it proved to be a small leak in the water main which crossed under our land. Other disasters, prone in an old neglected house, occurred. One day part of the chimney pot broke off and came down the chimney, covering the sitting room with soot, and even worse, a fragment of it fell down our neighbour's chimney, and she was not well pleased.

After living there for a year, it became possible for any one to build a new house. We knew that if we did not sell the house quickly and buy land to build, we would have great difficulty in selling our old terraced house. We were lucky and sold the house, although receiving much less for it than we had paid. While the new house was being built we lived with John's parents, and had the use of two rooms. Our new property was a modern detached house with a large garden. The land had been part of an estate, and a row of horse chestnut trees had flanked a drive, which now ran through the centre of the gardens. The trees had been felled but the huge stumps remained. One of our first outdoor jobs was to dig up the tree stump and roots, for it occupied a considerable part of the garden. My father in law and uncle came to help, and by levering and digging, the huge tree stump and root system was unearthed. The men viewed their work with satisfaction and pride, but then couldn't think how to get rid of it. It was far too big to carry through the side gate. They finally spent many more hours digging, until the hole was large enough to bury the stump and roots.

Before we were married we had been on holiday in Wales and the Lake District, and even managed to visit Scotland and stayed on the Isle of Bute. There we came across a very unusual organ in a village near where we were lodging, along the coast from Rothesay. After enjoying the day down by the sea and gaining permission to play the organ, the evenings were often spent at the church enjoying the music. It was a very eerie church, mainly due to the strange noises produced by the bellow's mechanism. It was powered by an hydraulic system, which creaked and groaned, but was very effective and saved me a lot of hard work. I have only come across one other organ using water to drive the bellows, and that was in Ireland. We enjoyed leaving the city and spending time in the countryside and by the sea, and these interludes kept our dreams and hopes alive.

One of the holidays that impressed us most of all, was spent staying with a family on Bardsey Island off the Lleyn peninsular in North Wales. The journey itself was quite an adventure. After travelling by train and bus, we arrived at the

Welsh coast at the Lleyn Peninsular, and continued our journey by a small motor boat which was buffeted by rough seas. We arrived safely, but then we were completely cut off from civilisation by a storm. The rough sea was unsuitable for the small motor boat, which was the only connection with the island. As a result of this we could send no letters or post cards for several days, and our parents were very worried, wondering what had happened. In those days very few ordinary families had telephones installed, so we could not let them know that we were safe. The family we stayed with had small children and the room that was allocated to me had a book case full of children's books. Among the books were several by A. A. Milne, I had never read them as a child, and was able to rectify my neglect, thoroughly enjoying them. There were only a few families on the island plus the lighthouse men. The school was very small, and teaching must have been difficult for some of the children only spoke the Welsh language, and the rest only English. The teacher was married to a Dutch man who was an artist, so I'm sure that the children enjoyed painting. We were made very welcome and joined in the activities of the community including bringing the harvest home. Although that holiday was over fifty years ago, I can remember that the island was over run with rabbits. They were not ordinary wild rabbits, but rabbits of various colours. Tame rabbits must have escaped at some time and bred with the wild population. I often wondered if they were wiped out when myxomatosis was introduced into the country in the early nineteen fifties, and devastated the rabbit population. Perhaps they escaped the devastation, living on an island. The fields were full of mushrooms, and one of the islanders collected baskets full early each morning, and weather permitting, took them across the sea to sell on the mainland. There was a small chapel on the island, but it was unused, for there was no one to take services there. The Sunday's we were there John lead a simple service. He was asked to baptise a baby, but was unable since he was not an ordained minister. Bardsey Island was a place of pilgrimage and the bones of many saints were buried there. Although it was little visited at that time, I believe that today it is quite an important place, as important as Iona and Lindisfarne, with accommodation for visitors. The island now has a welcome centre and a shop. That island holiday was our first real experience of island living, and kept our dreams and hopes alive.

When I married I gave up my work, as this was normal in the early nineteen fifties. We continued to serve in the church in varying capacities, but the way for full time church work did not materialise. I was bored, having given up my work, and our small terraced house required little housework to keep it in order. The education authority was approached, to see if it would be possible for me to train as a teacher. Unfortunately, this was not possible, although not many years later, schemes were initiated to allow mature students to train. The authority was helpful in suggesting that I might be able to teach in a private school, as they did not require a teaching diploma. They also gave me names of schools to contact in my area, where teachers were being sought. This resulted in my taking up part time posts in two schools. I had taken A level School Certificate in Chemistry, Biology, Physics and Mathematics, and these were the areas where there was a shortage of teachers, so I taught biology and maths. I enjoyed teaching biology part time in one school, and maths in another. My favourite subject was biology and I had started to study this subject at home with the idea of eventually taking a B.Sc. degree, for I regretted not going to university, but this ambition did not materialise for various reasons.

We could not afford a car so we both cycled. As our bicycles were getting old, we had the bright idea of buying a second hand tandem so that we could explore the countryside at weekends. It took some time to get used to the tandem, a different technique being needed. Our first efforts at riding it, gave much amusement to those watching us set off. After a few yards we both ended in a heap on the ground. The main trouble being that I instinctively steered instead of keeping my handlebars still, which resulted in disaster. The tandem proved to be heavy and needed a lot of energy, especially to cycle uphill. At that time small, two stroke petrol engines were becoming popular, and we purchased one. This was fitted at the front of the tandem and was a great success. We still needed to pedal hard on a steep hill, but the engine helped enormously. I remember one tandem outing was to Cannock Chase and there were lots of steep hills due to subsidence from the coal mines. I have walked regularly on the Chase in recent years, but it does not seem to bear any resemblance to the Chase I knew fifty years ago. Perhaps it has changed, or maybe my memory is incorrect.

One day I was in class at school and I was summoned to the head mistress's study. Apparently, John had called and needed to see me urgently. He was outside and I wondered what the trouble was. There was no trouble, just a very excited John who could not wait until I arrived home to show me what he had bought. Outside on the road was parked a second hand three wheeler car. This was our very first car. After the war several small cars appeared on the market. This was a Bond-Mini car, powered by a two stroke motor bike engine. It had no reverse and had to be lifted manually to turn it round when necessary. It only had two seats, both at the front, unlike the German three-wheeler, the Meschersmitt, which had two seats one behind the other. There were no doors, you just stepped over the side to reach the seats. When it was wet or cold a pram-like hood could be pulled over the top and fastened in place. We were young and agile, so had no difficulty in climbing over the side into the seat. John sometimes gave a lift to one of our neighbours and since he was much older and heavier than we were, he has been known to sit on the passenger's seat with his legs dangling over the side.

Our first long journey in the Bond was travelling to the Lake District to stay with friends. We wondered if our small car would get us there, but it did, although not without difficulties. The Lake District is a beautiful area with spectacular mountainous scenery. We were travelling to Loweswater, one of the smaller lakes, where we had friends who owned a farm. To get there we must drive over one of the mountain passes. Whinlatter Pass was very steep and we feared that the car would not have sufficient power to conquer the mountain with the weight of two people plus all the camping luggage. I volunteered to jump out and walk up the steep pass to lighten the load. After clambering out and giving the car a push, John dropped into bottom gear and I watched the small beetle like car making its way to the top of the pass. The hill was steep and I laboured up the mile to the top, while John waited at the summit with smoke rising from the overheated engine. It was a beautiful day and it was well worth the effort to enjoy the vista of green, rocky hills, with Loweswater shining as it nestled in the valley sheltered by the surrounding hills. I attempted to learn to drive in that three wheeler car, but gave up. The engine was started by pulling on a rope sharply. I found this very difficult and tiring, and on the few occasions I managed to start the engine it almost pulled me under the dash board. In addition to trying to maim me on starting, the engine became hot with my slow driving and then refused to switch off.

That first holiday after we were married marked the beginning of a new direction in our spiritual journey. We had both been brought up in the Brethren and had accepted their teaching. We had both stayed at school to take A levels in School Certificate, our chosen subjects being science and maths. We read widely and began to ask questions. We found it difficult to reconcile our church teaching with our scientific education. We needed explanations and became frustrated by being told that we must not question the teaching of the Bible but accept it as written by God, every word being infallible. Our study of the Bible aroused in us many questions and we were only allowed to use the Authorised Version. On purchasing modern translations and trying to find answers to our questions, we were in trouble with the church elders, and were told that we must accept everything by faith. We found it difficult to continue as members of the Brethren, yet we had been taught that other churches were not truly Christian, we finally left and tried to continue our spiritual lives alone, studying and worshipping together. Our faith was strong, but we felt lost, not knowing where to turn for help. Our holiday friends in the Lake District were Brethren Christians, and we were able to discuss our problems with them. Much to our surprise, they were very understanding and suggested that we should find a church near our home where they were sure that we would find fellowship and love. After the holiday we did this and became members of the nearest church, which happened to be a Baptist Church. During the short time we were members we made friends and were able to work and worship there. It was there that I became the church's representative for the Bible Society. Since those early days I have always taken an interest in and supported the Bible Society.

The Bond-Mini had a surprising amount of luggage space behind the seats. This came in very useful for the second holiday in the car which we planned to be a camping trip in Scotland. We poured over the map of Scotland for hours, looking for wild, rugged countryside running down to a rocky coast indented by sandy beaches, somewhere away from the usual holiday crowds. Eventually we decided to drive up to the South West of Scotland to the region called Galloway. Even this was too far to manage in one day, since our cruising speed was only 28 miles per hour, and we were setting off from the outskirts of Birmingham. The Bond had conquered the Lake District already, and we planned to break the journey there with our friends. The Bond did 90 miles to the gallon, but had many idiosyncrasies like refusing to start when the engine was hot, and this caused problems when we needed to fill up with petrol. The solution was to look for a petrol station on a hill, so that we could roll down the hill and engage the engine on the way down. It sometimes took several repeat performances, pushing the car back up the hill and then giving it a big push to give it momentum.

We intended to travel up to Scotland in the Bond and find a place on a farm where we could camp. We already possessed a tent, ground sheet, paraffin stove and all that we needed for camping, having spent an Easter weekend camping in mid Wales. On that occasion we had travelled by train carrying our equipment. This short holiday taught us many things. The weekend was hot and sunny by day, but very cold with a frost at night. That first night we lay on the ground sheet with our blankets around us, but could not sleep for the cold. We ended up fully clothed with the blankets wrapped around us sitting by the paraffin stove, trying to get warm. We almost came home, but the day was so hot and sunny and we did not want to waste our holiday. We collected armfuls of dead bracken from the hills around us and placed a thick layer beneath the ground sheet, this together with extra blankets lent to us by the farmer's wife, enabled us to stay and enjoy the holiday. This time we would carry more blankets and clothes in case the weather was cold. The car only had two seats, but the deep boot behind the seats, held all our camping gear with ease. We set out on our adventure and after a tedious journey through the chemical towns of the North

West of England, we arrived in the Lake District and spent the night at Loweswater. We set off early the next morning and eventually crossed into Scotland and through the unromantic looking village of Gretna Green. We were rather disappointed at this famous village, there was nothing attractive about it. The scenery changed as we passed through Dumfries into Galloway. We were heading for one of the coastal villages and drove along the coast road passing through the beautiful Shambellie estate not far out of Dumfries, heading for the south-west of Scotland. A private road ran through the estate, lined with beech trees which were in full leaf, forming a shady canopy through the woods. The ruined abbey at New Abbey needed exploring, but we were anxious to reach a destination where we could pitch our small tent, and continued on our way.

Food needed to be purchased, and we looked out for a village shop, and found one at Sandyhills along the coast road. To avoid stopping the engine, I jumped out at the village store, while John continued on to find a camp site. Sandyhills is noted for its long stretch of golden sands and now has a large, popular caravan park along the sand dunes. The messages were duly purchased and I waited patiently with the bags of shopping for the return of the Bond. It was hot and sticky, but since there was no car in sight I struggled along the road with my load. Still no sign of John, and I had reached a road turning. I did not know which way he had taken so sat at the side of the road anxiously waiting to be picked up. Of course, the problem was the usual one of an over heated engine. John switched off the engine to search for a place to camp, and the engine would not start again until it had cooled down.

This first Scottish holiday was in the early nineteen fifties, and there were few caravan sites in Scotland. A farmer gave us permission to camp on his field which over looked the sea. That holiday was idyllic. The sun shone each day out of a clear blue sky, the sea rolled in over the hot sands, and we spent much of the time in the warm water. We walked and explored the beautiful countryside around, climbed the cliffs and enjoyed the renown, golden sunsets as the sun sank behind the hills of Screel and Bengairn mirrored in the wet mud flats. The field where we were camping ran down to Rough Firth with its bird sanctuary island that belonged to the National Trust. We gazed at an island a few miles away, and looking through our telescope we could see that it had a small cottage and a lighthouse, and at least one person living there. As in the Lake District, the fields were divided off by stone walls. These, 'dry-stane dykes' were expertly built without mortar, the stones carefully sorted and piled up to make strong stable walls. In the evenings we sat on the dyke behind our tent drinking in the unbelievable beauty and peace of the place. This holiday was a great introduction to Galloway and we knew that we had found what we were looking for, this unspoiled, little known corner of Scotland was all for which we had hoped. Much of the following record of my journeying through life is associated with Galloway. Although, since then we have explored many areas of Scotland, and lived in several different places, Galloway has always held a special affection in my heart. John died twelve years ago, but if he had lived we would have retired to Galloway to spend the rest of our days together.

The following summer we returned to Galloway for another holiday. We still had our Bond-Mini but this time borrowed my father in law's car, so that the journey up would be quicker and less hazardous, and also we could explore more of the surrounding countryside. The dream of living in the country and making Scotland our home had not disappeared, and we decided to use this holiday to explore the possibilities. We camped on the same field, on Biggar's farm, which in these days boasts a large, well equipped caravan site. However, the weather was very different. The second night we decided to sleep in the car as it was so wet in and around the tent. To give us more room we placed our spare clothes and gear on the ground sheet inside the tent. We were woken by the sound of the heavy rain drumming on the car roof. I sat up in my sleeping bag and cleared the mist covered window, peering out in time to see a pair of shoes floating out of the tent on a stream that was flowing through the centre of the tent. Fortunately, our clothes were piled up on top of the ground sheet, and we were able to rescue our damp belongings before they became submerged in the water. The fun had gone out of camping as we surveyed the sodden field, the dripping tent and all our damp belongings. Enough was enough, the only sensible thing to do was to load our drenched equipment into the back of the car and make our way south and home.

The previous year we had attended the local church and made friends with the minister and his wife, and John was given permission to play the organ. On arriving in Galloway we had popped in to tell them we were back for another holiday, and had been invited to visit them. The car was loaded and ready to set off, and on the way we called at the manse to say goodbye and tell them that as everything was so wet camping was impossible and we were travelling home. The forecast was poor and it was prudent to return home and dry out. Our new friends would not hear of this, they invited us to stay at the manse for a few days, for they felt sure that in a day or two the rain would be replaced by sunshine. This proved to be true and we were able to resume our camping. This stay at the manse proved to be a landmark on our journey, and the beginning of some of our many dreams being fulfilled.

Chapter 2 **A Dream Fulfilled.**

"For surely I know the plans I have for you, says the Lord, plans for your wel-
fare and not for harm, to give you a future with hope." (Jeremiah ch. 29 v. 11.)

Our two days staying at the manse with Elsie and Edward Jack, were very enjoyable for they were very hospitable. We had time to talk to them about our hopes
and dreams, especially moving to Scotland and living in the country. They were
able to advise us on local properties for sale and the likely cost. The purchase
of property had to be accompanied by the means of earning a living. All his life
John had been fascinated by pipe organs. Our cycling trips into the country usually ending with a church visit and seeking permission to play the organ. When
he left school, unable to take up organ building as a trade, he did an apprenticeship in production and mechanical engineering, which led to a good job in
research at Dunlop. After reading many books about church organs, John started to build himself a pipe organ as a hobby. Building pipe organs or farming
were ideas we had for earning a living. Our searching turned out to be fruitless
for properties proved to be far more expensive than we could afford and there
was little hope of obtaining employment.

Since leaving the Brethren our spiritual journey seemed uneventful. We enjoyed
worshipping and serving in our new church, but we felt that our future did not
belong there. We had prayed earnestly for guidance, but were well aware of the
difficulties in planning ahead. I still find seeking guidance very difficult; our
own wants and desires so colour what we believe is guidance by God. We also
had learned that God had given us common sense, gifts, imagination and
strengths, all of which should be used in seeking the way ahead. I have encountered many Christians who believe that God will open doors for us if we will
only sit back waiting, doing nothing and leaving everything to him. That may
be the right way for some, but I believe that opportunities can be missed if we
sit back and are unable to take responsibility, waiting for decisions to be forced
upon us. God has given us brains, insight and vision to be used, as long as we
acknowledge that all are from God to be used to his glory.

One night during our stay at the manse Elsie mentioned that the tenant who lived
on Heston Island, the island we had gazed on longingly the previous summer,
was thinking about leaving. He was an old man and lived there alone, looking
after the lighthouse, and wintering sheep, and his relatives were worried about
him, and were trying to persuade him to leave. They could see our eagerness at
this news, and tried to dampen our enthusiasm by pointing out all its short com-
ings. There was no electricity, gas or mains water. Every thing had to be trans-

ported on to the island by boat and sometimes no one could get on or off the island because of high tides and strong winds which whipped up the sea, making it impossible for small boats, and difficult even for larger boats to land. The cottage was small and in a terrible condition, and there was no anchorage, any boat must be small enough to be manhandled up the steep shingle beach. This limited independent transport to and from the island, since a boat small enough to be lifted out of the sea's destructive forces, would not be safe in rough seas. All the negative arguments against living on Heston island were listened to, but they did not dampen our enthusiasm. This was our first glimmer of hope and we intended to pursue it.

The rain cleared, we had dried out, and we returned to our camping holiday. We decided to get as close to the island as possible and have a really good look through our telescope. The nearest land to the island was Almorness Point, and at that time there were no tracks down to the head of the peninsular. Nowadays, that area has been cleared and planted with trees, and the Forestry Commission has made tracks quite close to the point. Undeterred, we skirted the bogs by struggling through the forest of bracken, which was way above our heads. We pushed through brambles and heather to clamber over the rocks to the hill opposite Heston. We had a good view of the island across quite a short stretch of water, and it looked even more desirable from this distance. Had we known, we could have walked across to Heston from Almorness point at low tide.

Later we discovered that fishermen from the next village regularly took their motor boat to the island, arriving as the tide went out so that they could pick mussels from the rack of rocks, which had built up from the island. The rough seas whirling round islands form strong currents which move rocks, stones and mud and build up causeways which stretch out from the islands, sometimes joining them to the mainland. Heston's causeway, or rack, stretched about three-quarters of the way towards the Almorness point, and at low tide the rest of the way was firm sand. Almorness Point was the southern most point of Glenisle. There was a stretch of inaccessible bog land between the Point and the nearest remote farm, and even that farm was cut off at high tides as the sea poured over the flat narrow strip of land beyond the farm. The fishermen made extra money by taking visitors over to Heston and leaving them there to explore while they picked mussels. No one could leave until the tide came up and there was enough water to steer through the channels that had been cut out by the fast flowing River Urr. The men lived at Kippford, a village about three or four miles from Rockcliffe by road, but only a mile by the cliff path.

Kippford was the local centre for sailing, and we had discovered it the previous year by walking over the cliff path. We had little experience of the sea, our only adventure being the rough trip over to Bardsey Island in a small motor boat, and the occasional messing about in boats on the pool in the local park. We walked over to Kippford, enjoying the wonderful view of the Urr estuary, the water reflecting the sunlight, as dozens of small boats danced on their moorings as the tide turned and began to flow out. The small village stretched along the road with some houses built up on the hillside. The peninsular of Glenisle ending in the Almorness Point could be clearly seen. The flat meadow beyond the farm was narrow and would easily be flooded by the tide. Glenisle was often truly an island. The coast line beyond Glenisle was rugged in places, but curved into two beautiful, sandy bays. Only Horse Isles bay could be seen from the cliff path, White Port bay lay hidden. Both these sandy bays were very popular with the sailing community, for in those days they could only be easily reached by sea. The locals say that the river writes its name in the mud flats, and certainly the channels have many bends and dead ends. Later we were to discover the dangers and problems of the river on our first trip out to Heston in our own very new dinghy.

At high tide the channels were completely hidden, with several feet of water covering them. There were many sand banks on the estuary, making it imperative that sailors were aware of the dangers lying beneath the water. The thick layer of mud left exposed at low tide on the Solway estuary, was covered with a layer of sand and was firm enough for walking on in many places. This was not so at Kippford where the river had scoured out a deep channel and at low tide soft, glutinous mud and steep mud banks lined the river. It was the sort of mud that readily sucked off your wellington boots. Later, I sampled the sticky Kippford mud when anchoring our dinghy. Fortunately, I was wearing old clothes, and the water hoses on the Yacht Club's jetty give a powerful jet of water to wash away the mud. Years later, when we were holidaying, our own children thoroughly enjoyed themselves in the Kippford mud, and needed to be hosed down before we could take them in the car to the campsite showers.

We managed to contact the fishermen and arranged to travel with them to Heston on the next day. There were only two men, the third fisherman was very ill and died not long after, and we never met him. Kippford is a picturesque village lying two or three miles inland from the sea, at the head of Rough Firth. It used to be a fishing village, but is now noted as the centre of the yachting community in that part of Galloway. Higher up the river is the village of Palnackie, and when we were there, ships regularly manoeuvred their way up the river at high tide and unloaded fertiliser, taking back a load of Galloway timber to Holland. Much of Galloway is blanketed in coniferous forests. Although they have their attraction, the purists bemoan the passing of the old open moor lands, and deciduous woods. In the old days, the ships managed to reach the town of Dalbeattie, and relics of mooring posts can still be seen along the river banks. Because the Solway tides are huge, the whole of Rough firth dries out at low tide, the boats looking like stranded whales as they lie awkwardly on the mud banks. Only those moored in the river channel remained upright.

The men were very familiar with the river's channels, for they motored out to Heston about three hours before low tide, when the water had dropped sufficiently to reveal the channels, but still with enough water for their fishing boats. The low tide revealed the maze of intricate channels, some no longer used and silted up, as new channels had been scoured out by the power of the water. They returned as soon as there was enough water for the boat to float, so again needed to navigate through the channels. They were out on the rack for about four hours, plenty long enough for the back breaking, difficult task of removing the mussels one by one from the rocks. We set out with our picnic and the journey took just under half an hour. Heston was four miles from Kippford, but the route out at that state of the tide was tortuous. We landed on the rack and made our way up to the steep path leading to the cottage and the rest of the island.

Heston covers about thirty acres of rough grass land and is surrounded by cliffs, except at the north end which is a steep bank of shingle leading down to the rack. The southern cliffs are steep and boast a cave, made famous by the book "The Raiders" written by the nineteenth century author S. R. Crockett. On the western side there is a cove, Copper Cove, where there are man made caves, bored out of the cliff to mine copper. There proved to be insufficient copper on the island to make it worth while installing the equipment needed. Copper was mined on the mainland cliffs, west of Heston, and remnants of the old mines can be found. The cove has access from a steep cliff track, and many years ago the only drinking water available to the island was from a pool of fresh water in one of the caves. We explored the whole island, climbing up the steep path to the small lighthouse, lit then by acetylene gas formed by dripping water onto lime. The south of the island was the breeding place of seagulls and terns and there was much guano deposited on the cliff ledges and the flat, tern nesting site. The air was filled with the cries of the seagulls and the creaking calls of the terns who swooped over our heads as we climbed the hill towards the south of the island. We plucked up courage and called on the tenant, Mr. Houston. He was a gaunt old man, shabbily dressed, and at his side was an old sheep dog, but he was obviously a well educated Scot. When we mentioned that we had heard that he might be leaving the island, he bristled and denied that that was his intention. However, he did mellow a little later on when we told him our dream of living on an island, and promised to let us know if he did decide to move back to the mainland. We continued to read the local paper for news of properties for sale, and drove around the area looking at properties, but none were within our price range. Our holiday was over, and we returned home without finding anywhere to live in Galloway. We had a flicker of hope and nursed a dream that perhaps an island life might be possible after all.

Those first few months after returning home and back to work were filled with dreams and an eager expectancy of hearing from Mr. Houston, who was not only the tenant, but also half owner of the island. We made enquiries of the solicitors who handled the property, and were told that the island belonged to several members of the Houston family. Owning part of the island was prestigious, and there was no hope of any of the family wanting to sell the island. We heard nothing and began to lose hope, but in early spring of 1957 we received a letter. It seemed that there was a possibility of a new tenant, and we would definitely be considered. Later we were ecstatic on hearing the news, that if we wanted, we could take on the tenancy of Heston Island from May 28th 1957. We contacted Mr. Houston with our letter of acceptance, and received an invitation to stay on the island with him for a few days. This was to show us round and instruct us with regard to the lighthouse duties. Arrangements were made for us to visit for a week in April, and we contacted the fishermen to transport us and our sleeping bags etc. to the island. On our holidays we had talked to many of the local people, and Mrs. Edwards, who ran the village shop, was very kind and helpful. We bought the food that we should need from her store, and were even lent cutlery in case we needed it.

The inside of the cottage came as a bit of a shock, the old man was a bachelor, and obviously was not used to housework. He had made an effort for our coming and told us that he had bought some new cushion covers. Every where was covered with piles of dusty old books, including hundreds of paper back western novels. The bit of table where we were to eat was hastily brushed free of dead flies. The cottage had the one large sitting room heated by an old cast iron hob, which was used for all the cooking. There was a small bedroom off the sitting room where Mr. Houston slept. A short corridor led from the sitting room to another bedroom, which was heated by a wrought iron closed stove. This was the room we had been given and was furnished with a double bed. We had brought our own sleeping bags. Onto this stone cottage, a wooden lean-to kitchen, with a corrugated iron roof, had been added. Another similar structure had been built at the front of the cottage and was divided into two small rooms, both of them filled with junk, including hundreds of empty evaporated milk tins. Mr. Houston told us that he was saving these to build into his small boat to make

21

a buoyancy tank. Since each can was pieced in two places to allow the milk out, it would have been a mammoth task to solder up the holes before using the tins, and the cans would soon corrode in the salt water. We were shown the lighthouse and told our responsibilities for it. The sheep wintered on the island until the end of May, and one of our jobs would be to count them each day to make sure that none of them were in difficulty. He impressed on us very strongly to always use the village of Kippford as our mainland contact, and never to attempt to walk off the island. At low tide the whole of the mud flats on the west side of the island was a 'quarking qua'. By this we understood that it was an area of quick sands where people had lost their lives.

It was quite an experience staying on the island. Mr. Houston, having explained what was expected of us as island tenants, left us entirely to ourselves. He seemed to have no concept of time, getting up and going to bed at any hour. He had just one meal a day, which consisted of a whole large loaf of bread cut into thick slices, a pan full of bacon cooked on the range until it was black charcoal, and some jam. The first day, he left his bacon cooking while he went up to the light house to do a job. I moved it to the side of the stove as it had begun to burn. On returning he pushed the blackened pan back onto the fire, and waited till all the bacon was charcoal, and then ate it with relish. He remarked that modern housewives were wasteful and did not know how to be thrifty. He made his pot of jam last twice as long by mixing it with an equal amount of boiling water. He put a spoonful of the watered down jam into his mouth and then dipped the spoon back into the jar and offered me a spoonful to taste! Mr. Houston had trained as a lawyer, but never practised, and seemed a bit of a recluse. When he first came to Heston a friend lived with him, but the friend found it too remote and lonely and soon left.

While we were there we decided to work on the two walled gardens. They were overgrown, but one had a good patch of rhubarb. We fertilised the ground with sea weed, carrying up load after load on an old hand barrow. It was very hard work, but we were full of enthusiasm and looked forward to harvesting a good crop later that year. We had brought with us seeds, and planted lettuce, radishes, sea-kale and carrots and one of the gardens we reserved for potatoes. We had plenty of time to savour the peace of the island, to sit on the cliffs above the cottage and watch the occasional yachtsman skimming through the sea with colourful sails filled with the wind. The fishermen came each day, and were bent double filling their sacks with mussels. At the south end of the island the waves crashed against the cliffs filling the air with spray, and the gulls wheeled and turned, glinting in the sun as they dived into the sea. Our visit soon came to an end and we said our goodbyes and returned to the mainland with the fishermen, and started our long drive home.

We were filled with hope for our island future and were already making our plans and wanting the time to hasten on so that we could begin our new life. The period leading up to our move to Scotland was a hectic time with many personal problems to be resolved, but above all we needed to have a plan for the future. During the holidays we had spent in the Lake District with friends, we had helped out on the farm, but we knew we were very inexperienced and had much to learn if we were going to make a living from the island. On my free time from teaching, while John was at work, I would visit our local library and bring home books on farming. Our hope was that we would be able to farm the island, and we studied crop rotation, and what crops we would need to grow to feed any animals we decided to keep. We had a demonstration of a two wheeled tractor. Anything larger would be difficult to use on Heston's sloping hillside. In the event we were unable to put much of the study to use, but it was good to be planning for the future.

Now our dream of renting Heston had been fulfilled, our first real task was to put our home on the market. Selling our house was easier than we had expected. We sold it quickly and had to turn away a number of prospective buyers. John had given in his notice at work and I had finished my last term at school. The electrical equipment we owned would be of no use on Heston, and we gave it away. Everything was going well, even the removers were booked . A short time before we were due to leave, the young couple who were buying our house arrived. The girl was in tears. Their own house sale had dropped through at the last minute and they had to withdraw from buying our house. So we were left with an unsold property on our hands as we started off on our new life. After paying off the mortgage, together with the money we had managed to save, we hoped that we would have about a £1000 left as capital. We intended to invest half of our capital in a building society, and the rest would buy a boat, an outboard motor and all the equipment we needed, with enough left over for us to use until we began to make a living. The loss of the sale was a great blow, especially as when we put the house up for sale the second time, nobody seemed interested. By the time the house was sold we were settled on the island.

We had a long slow journey ahead of us in the Bond, but we set out early. John's mother and aunt had volunteered to stay at the house and supervise the loading of our furniture and belongings. They also promised to look after our property and keep it in good condition until it was sold. The weather was good and we had an uneventful journey to Scotland and pitched our tent for the night and were ready for the removal van to arrive the next day. The evening was warm and fine and we camped where we could look across to our island. Less than two years previously we had looked with envy and longing, wondering who lived there, and if we would ever be lucky enough to live on an island. It was a time to savour the wonder of it all. Over there the cottage was waiting for us and we hoped our crops were growing well. We thanked God that another of our dreams was about to be fulfilled although we were aware that our house was unsold, we had very little money in the bank, and our furniture was somewhere on the road to Kippford. But nothing could spoil the moment as we watched the sunset over Bengairn. As we settled into our sleeping bags we again thanked God and asked for his provision and protection and the fulfilment of the hopes we had for the future.

The villagers were very friendly and wanted to help. The Ellender family let cottages in the summer and had a large garage. They kindly offered the garage to us for storing the furniture when it arrived. The first part of the removal was the easy part, even though it was a two hundred and fifty mile trip. We expected the flitting to the island to take several days as the fishermen would only agreed to carry our belongings over on their usual daily mussel trip. They had mussel contracts to fulfil, and needed to keep to their usual time table. Our tent was pitched for our stay in Kippford while the furniture was transported over to the island, but the Ellenders insisted that we used the facilities of one of their holiday cottages, and we accepted their kindness willingly.

Chapter 3 Sea Flitting.

"Go in peace. The mission you are on is under the eye of the Lord."   (Judges ch. 18 v.6)

Galloway is in the west and can be very wet, as we had experienced on our second holiday. There is a local saying, that if you can see the Isle of Man then it is going to rain. If you cannot see the Isle of Man, then it is raining already. We knew that if the weather were bad, we could end up with very soggy furniture. Our Father God answered our prayers that week, and every day dawned bright and dry. Each day the furniture, stored in the garage, was transported to the village jetty, a distance of about 400 yards, and left piled up ready for the fishermen to load. We were lucky enough to borrow a boat trailer from the yacht club, and this facilitated the work. The weather was absolutely ideal, it was dry and sunny, although there was quite a chop on the sea and this almost proved to be a disaster on one day. The fishermen used their thirty foot boat to transport our furniture and timed their departure so that the tide had dropped sufficiently for them to navigate down the estuary and through the channels. They stowed the first load of furniture aboard, the sea calm and still, and set off to arrive at Heston as the tide left the mussel beds. The first part of the journey was sheltered and we had no problems. As we came out of the shelter a brisk breeze hit us and the boat rolled in the swell and we held on to the furniture as it began to shift with the sea's movement. It was good to arrive at our destination with the strain of the sea voyage over so that we could relax a little, but not for long. The water had left the rack and we heaved the furniture and boxes out of the boat. We had three or four hours to carry all of it up the steep path before the tide returned and washed over the rack. It was hard work, and we needed to pause often to regain our breath.

Much to our surprise old Mr. Houston had not left the island, and he was still packing his bits and pieces and seemed to have no intention of leaving that day. Our first job was to clean out one of the byres so that we could stack the furniture there. It was soon time for the return journey with the fishermen, and it was good to relax and cook a meal in the holiday cottage before we thankfully retired to bed, exhausted by our first day of flitting by sea. The morning soon arrived and once again we struggled down to the jetty with the days allocation of belongings. None of us were trained in the art of removal packing, and it was all a bit haphazard. The loaded boat motored out of the shelter of the land and a stiff breeze hit us again. The wind was from the east and a sharp white- crested chop had built up on the sea. The Solway Firth has a reputation of fast tides and quick sands and can be very dangerous higher up the firth where the Solway narrows to Dumfries and Annan. There have been many lives lost. Out by Heston, the Solway is somewhat tamed by the open sea. There are many miles of level sand banks and these make the seas short and choppy. In a full gale the crashing of the breakers over these banks is a most impressive sight.

The news of a young couple moving onto Heston Island had spread. One day as we were waiting for the load to be stacked aboard Fred's boat a newspaper reporter arrived. This was the first time we had ever encountered a newspaper man, and this was the first and the best of many interviews that occurred when we were settled on the island. A sensible and accurate account of our venture appeared in the local paper the following week. Those reporters who descended on us when we were installed on Heston used much more imagination. Headings such as "Childhood Sweethearts on Smugglers' Isle" hit the papers. The fishermen would not make special trips to Heston, so anyone wanting to come out to interview us had to fit in with the mussel picking. As a result they had several hours on the island, and became a nuisance, getting under our feet when we were anxious to make the cottage habitable and the byres weather proof. When the man from the Daily Mail arrived I hardly spoke to him, but he made up for my silence by printing imaginary quotes.

On the third day of our furniture ferrying trip over to the island, we had quite an unusual conversation with one of the fishermen. We thought at first that he was having us on, but later realised that he was sounding us out. "A gran place, Heston. Aye, a gran place. Quiet ye ken. Aye quiet." A long silence followed and then he spoke again showing signs of enthusiasm. "There's some bonny caves on Heston." We agreed and wondered where the conversation was leading, usually very little was said on our trips. "Ye could set up a still on Heston, an' naebody the wiser." We laughed, not really knowing if this was a joke or not. He then lowered his voice and said "Ah could get rid o' ony quantity, ye ken. Ony quantity." We laughed again, and the message delivered, he sat back and reverted to his usual silence. Back in the cottage we reflected on what had been said, and wondered if he was really suggesting that we should set up a still in one of the caves. We were city folk and knew nothing about elicit alcohol or smuggling, except for adventure stories read in books. In the light of something that happened later, when we returned to Heston from a weekend away, we realised that he was sounding us out, sowing the seed perhaps for later.
That week was very tiring as we wheeled the boat trailer piled up precariously with our belongings to the jetty each day, helped to stow it on board, unloaded it on the rack, and then the back breaking work of carrying it up the steep hill and storing it in the byre. We returned to the holiday cottage after each trip tired but happy as we could see our belongings safely stored in our future home. On

the way home, one day, we were extremely surprised to see Jeff manhandle one of the painfully filled mussel sacks, to the edge of the boat and tipped its contents overboard. We could not help showing our amazement at this bizarre behaviour of throwing away the fruits of hours of painful work, so they explained to us why they were acting in such an odd way. They had had a good day at the picking, and the mussels dropped overboard were surplus to their requirements. They knew exactly where they had jettisoned the load which was on the top of a sand bank. When they had a poor day they would rescue the mussels and make up the weight they needed. There would not be time for the mussels to cling to any rocks or stones, so they could easily be scooped up again. They not only sold their mussels for consumption, but also had a contract to supply the 'Nuclear Authority', and these were tested for signs of radiation. Any nuclear pollution entering the sea from Selafield, could be detected in the mussels. On another occasion when we were travelling off with the men to Kippford, we again saw them dump a sack of mussels back into the sea, and the visitors being conveyed back to Kippford were astounded, but were too polite to question the men about their action.

The wind seemed to be increasing each day, and on the fifth day, Jeff decided to take both their boats and finish the furniture removal, in case a gale was coming. On this trip John and I were both together in Jeff's boat, Fred was alone in the second boat. As we came out of the sheltered estuary the wind hit us and the boats began to dig into the waves. We looked across to Fred, and to our horror we saw him leave the tiller to its own devices while he grappled with our mattress which had been dislodged and was just about to disappear overboard. We were not near enough to help, but fortunately, Fred's wrestling with the mattress was rewarded, and our vision of having no mattress, or at the best a soggy one, was unfounded.

This was our last trip and we would not be going back to the mainland, but spending our first night as tenants on the island. Old Mr. Houston was still in the cottage and seemed reluctant to leave. We pitched our small tent ready for the night, and cleared out another byre where we could cook our food and live for some days, as we knew that we needed to carry out a lot of cleaning in the cottage before we moved in. First of all we had to take over the tenancy of the cottage, and see the previous tenant safely off the island. Mr. Houston had bought a caravan as temporary accommodation until he was able to buy a cottage. We helped him finish his last bit of packing and loaded it onto his boat. Much to our surprise this included a sack of old bread crusts growing a mould, but he insisted on taking it, he never wasted food he assured us. John saw him aboard and started his outboard motor and set him on his way. We watched him until he was safely across the open sea and into the shelter of the land, and out of our sight.

Now we needed to start the next difficult part of our new beginning. The cottage was in such a state that we thought it wise to fumigate the property and had brought with us sulphur candles for the job. We then needed to leave the cottage open to get rid of the sulphur smell. This meant that we had to continue to camp out for a while yet. We were still blessed with fine, sunny weather, and spent this time clearing out the outhouses. John intended to fulfil his dream of building pipe organs, and we needed to clean out the barns on the far side of the cottage and mend the roofs. Later it was reported to us that the gossip spreading in the village was that we were going to Heston to grow orchids. I suppose organs and orchids are words that sound a little alike, and passing from one to another by word of mouth the mistake easily occurred.

Heston was well known for its large population of gulls. Some years, as well as large areas of nesting gulls, terns also nested. The fishermen had told us that during the war when eggs were in short supply they had gathered seagull eggs, and when they were fresh they were very good to eat. We intended to be as self sufficient as possible on our island, and as it was the nesting season we decided we would sample the eggs. It was possible to test the eggs to see if they were fresh by putting them in salt water. If they floated, then they were not fresh and we discarded them. There were masses of eggs, and we selected four fresh ones to make a large omelette. The colour was a much deeper yellow than hen's eggs, but it tasted good. There was no fishy taste, just egg. What I had forgotten was that the seagull's eggs were two or three times as big as a hen's egg. Before we were half way through the omelette we had had more than enough, and could eat no more. I don't think that I ever used the eggs to make omelettes again, but they were used in other ways, especially in baking, with very good results. Eddie, the salmon fisherman from Auchencairn, whom we came to know later, recounted a story of the popularity of a baker in Castle Douglas during the war. One spring his shop was well stocked with lovely cakes, when the other shops were restricted by the shortage of eggs and fat. Eddie had found a barrel of lard washed up on the Heston shore and sold it, together with large quantities of gulls' eggs to the baker. That spring the baker produced a variety of cakes and goodies, to the envy and unbelief of the other shopkeepers in the area, who had to rely on their meagre rations.

That first night on our own island was magical. During the war in the blackout, we had enjoyed night walks in the dark looking at the undimmed beauty of the starry skies. After the war the lights of the towns spoiled the full glory of the night sky. Now, here we were miles from any town and able to enjoy again the wonder of the jewel spangled skies, listen to the lapping of the water on the shore below the cottage, and climb up to the southern cliffs and see the shimmering of the reflected moonlight on the dark undulating water, with the salty taste of the spray on our lips as the waves dashed against the cliffs. This was a very spiritual experience for me and I was reminded of it when I was visiting New Zealand a year ago. I stayed at Te Anau on the South Island and there experienced another star spangled sky which again was a wonderful spiritual experience of God's wonderful universe. This was a grotto deep inside a cave system. We had travelled over the lake and then pushed through the caves on a punt and witnessed under groundwater falls and stalactites, finally reaching the inner cave. We sat there in complete silence looking up at a myriad of glow worms shining from the blackness of the cave's roof. Although there were a number of people sitting in that boat, I felt that I was the only one there surrounded by God's presence and love.

That night as we settled into our sleeping bags we thanked God for safely bringing us to the island of our dreams, and for his protection and love. As I look back to that night forty-five years ago, I again thank God for his many blessings throughout our lives, not only for the journey and guidance in our secular lives, but especially for the many blessings in our spiritual journey.

Chapter 4 **Settling in.**

"My people will live in peaceful dwelling places, in secure homes." (Isaiah ch. 32 verse 18)

At last we were in our own home again. Admittedly, we were still camping out, but we were now ensconced on Heston, no more trailing across the water each day, praying for a good safe journey on the following day. We had travelled to and from the island with the mussel fisherman, and of necessity fitted in with their time schedule. Once we became tenants we needed to be independent, and have our own transport. Mr. Houston had instilled into us that we must not try to walk across the mud flats to the west, because of the quick sands between the island and Balcary Bay on the mainland. It was, therefore, necessary for us to buy a boat. Before moving to Scotland we had ordered a boat and an outboard motor. Fibreglass was the new material now being used to build boats, and our 14 foot dinghy had a double hull so that if the outer hull were damaged the dinghy would still float. The joy of fibre glass, we were told, was that the boat never needs painting or repairing. While we were still moving our furniture on to the island, we heard that our boat had arrived and was waiting for collection at the station in Dalbeattie. It was good to have a break from furniture removing and we made a trip into Dalbeattie to see the boat and arrange for its delivery. It was still in its transport cradle and looked huge to us. On its arrival at Kippford, we watched its unloading onto the beach. The outboard motor had not arrived, but this gave us opportunity to practise rowing in the calm waters of the estuary. The fishermen enjoyed shouting instructions to us as we revealed our incompetency with the oars. When we moved on to Heston our boat was towed out to us on one of the mussel picking trips. Although it was quite heavy we managed to haul it up to the top of the pebble beach out of harm from the tide. A strong rope and a 12lb fisherman's anchor were attached. We soon discovered that there was quite a difference between rowing a boat on the calm estuary and on the choppy surface of the sea.

One day as a break from the back-aching work of cleaning and repairing, John decided that he was accomplished enough to row out a little and try his hand at fishing. I helped him push off from the shore and watched him row out and drop the anchor and bait the hook with mussel to start his fishing. From time to time I looked out, but there didn't seem to be much activity going on in the boat. There was little sign of fishing, and John appeared to be lying down in the boat having a nap. I began to be worried and went down to the shore to see what was wrong. He heard me calling and then rowed back to the shore, looking decidedly worse for wear. Although it was a calm day there was a swell on the sea which caused the anchored dinghy to sway gently up and down. After a while John began to feel very unwell and all thought of catching fish disappeared. He wanted to row back to the shore, but it was quite sometime before he felt capable of getting the anchor up and grabbing the oars to row. I can't remember John ever going out in the boat again to fish off Heston; although years later he often went out fishing on Loch Fyne and caught lots of fish. That first experience prevented him from trying again while we were on Heston, and we probably missed many a fish meal. Our fishing was not a sport, but a necessity in providing food. Later, when we were living near Loch Fyne in Argyll we were always saddened to see boats setting off to catch fish for sport, and bringing back loads of fish which were often thrown away for no one required them. God has made us stewards of our planet and provided food and resources for our needs, but we often misuse or waste the resources provided for us.

After we had been on the island a fortnight, Fred delivered the outboard motor. It was an eventful day for us, for now we could be independent and leave the island whenever we wanted, providing the weather was suitable. No longer would we have to depend on the fishermen to bring out our food. John had had some experience with small petrol engines. We had fitted a two-stroke engine to our tandem when we were first married. As already described, we then graduated to our first small car, a three wheeled Bond with a motor bike engine. This engine had many idiosyncracies, but John eventually conquered it. I never overcame the peculiar behaviour of our first car. The experience of being pulled under the dash board on starting it, unnerved me, and I was quite content to let John struggle with its perverse nature. In the years he drove the Bond, John became very familiar with all the secrets of that particular engine, including the difficulties of starting it when it was hot. John's delight was plain to be seen as he unpacked the clean, shining motor from its wooden case. He read all the instructions carefully, filled up the tank with petrol and fixed the motor to the boat. The instructions seemed to be clear enough, but seemed to involve having more than two hands, for in addition to pulling the starter rope the carburettor intake had to be closed and the throttle operated. In spite of the initial difficulties, which at first seemed insurmountable, John eventually conquered it. This small motor was very reliable and lasted for very many years. In fact it was the most reliable motor that he ever bought.

Our first trip back to Kippford from Heston, proudly using our own transport, was in the company of the fishermen. We followed them to the mainland to learn the route, as once we entered the estuary the channels were tortuous. We anchored the dinghy, which very soon became high and dry on the sloping mud flats, and drove off in our Bond-Mini to do a large shopping. We could not set

31

back for Heston until the tide returned, and there was sufficient water in the river channel for us to lower the outboard motor. We reckoned that there would probably be enough water for us to start the engine well before ten o'clock that night. Before we moved onto the island we bought a tide-table, for hence forth our lives would revolve round the tides not the clock. The tide was coming in fast, the water pouring in and rushing up the channel and we hauled the dinghy into the water, loaded in our shopping and climbed aboard. We gingerly lowered the motor and started it up. The motor bumped ominously on the rocks beneath us, and we quickly hauled it up to safety. There was not sufficient water to clear the rocks, and we were in danger of damaging the propeller. As the outboard motor was secured, I hastily dropped the anchor overboard, for already the strong current was sweeping us backwards up the river. There was nothing for it, but to sit in the boat and wait until the tide rose sufficiently to give a good depth of water over the rocks. In about ten minutes we tried again, but with the same disastrous results. By this time it was getting dark. It was eleven o'clock before we set off, and the only light was the faint green afterglow in the northern sky which showed us the dim outline of the coast and mud banks. That was our first journey back to Heston in our own boat, and one that I will never forget for it was a nightmare. In the darkness it was very difficult to distinguish between the water and the edge of the mud banks. John had learned the route and when he thought we had travelled far enough he turned into the channel which would lead us towards Gibb's Hole woods, which we could dimly see in the distance. What he had not taken into consideration was that we were travelling at a much slower rate than Fred's thirty foot boat. Again we turned south after a period which we reckoned would be about right, only to run into a steep mud bank. The engine stalled and we tried to puzzle out where we were. This channel that had led us to a dead end, was one of the old silted up channels. We had no idea where we were, for we had thought that we were in the correct channel that would lead us out to the open sea. It was very dark and we could not remember ever having noticed this channel. The engine had cut out in the panic of the emergency and now there was the difficult job of restarting it. Once the engine was running again we made our way back down the channel wondering how we could find the correct route and find our way out of this maze. It was late, we were on our own and could ask no one's help. We made our way slowly, sometimes scraping the bottom and churning up the mud. We could see the village of Rockcliffe about a mile away, but were aware that no one knew that we were out there on the sea feeling utterly lonely, and wondering if we would ever find our way back to our island home.

It was a worrying and frustrating situation and we wondered whether it would be best to drop anchor and sit for about three hours, waiting for the tide to cover all the mud banks. There would then be no need for us to worry about finding the right channels to lead us out of the estuary into the open sea, and we would not need to struggle against the currents. This was the last resort and we did not have to take it for our prayers were answered, and we avoided the long cold wait on the rising tide. By trial and error we slowly found our way out of the blind channels and into the main channel leading to Gibb's Hole pool. It was necessary for us to follow the coast line for a little way, but to keep sufficiently far out from the rocks that jutted out from the cliffs. We were then able to make our way out to the open sea, again keeping well clear of any outcrops of rocks. It was not far off midnight and the current at this point of the tide was fast and the journey out from Gibb's Hole seemed interminably slow. As we came round Horse Isles the welcoming flash of the Heston light greeted us, and we knew we were only about a mile from home and could point the bow towards the light. When the lighthouse flashes disappeared we would be under the cliffs and only a short way from the shore. It was after midnight when we felt the crunching of the shells under the hull and cut the motor having arrived home safely. The boat was half dragged and lifted up the bank of shells and pebbles until it was out of the reach of the tide, and we made our weary way up to the cottage. The Tilley lamp was soon lit, giving out warmth and comfort as it gently hissed, and we made a hot drink before crawling into our safe comfortable bed, giving thanks for our safe return. Much later, after we came to know the people of Rockcliffe, we discovered that some of the villagers had been aware of our hazardous trip, and eyes had been scanning the sea as they watched until the light in the cottage came on, and they knew that we were safely home.

There was only one cottage on the island which covered an area of about 30 acres, and except for the north end, which sloped steeply down to a pebbly beach, the island was surrounded by steep cliffs. From the mainland Heston looked like a large stranded whale. It was a third of a mile long and a quarter of a mile wide. The cliffs surrounding the island were about a hundred feet high, and there were about ten acres of cliff and rocks above the high tide mark, dropping steeply down from the hill side. The cliffs were composed of crumbling rock and in the pockets of soil, grass, brambles and briars grew among the rocks in profusion. There were twenty two acres of land at the top of the island, which had a good depth of rich soil covered by grass and bracken. The island sloped upwards, towards a fairly flat area near the light house. This was a favourite nesting site for the common tern, and the first year we saw sandwich terns nesting there. The sandwich terns differed from the common tern in the colour of their beaks. Instead of red beaks tipped with black, their beaks were black tipped with yellow. They were the shape of swallows and swifts, and their call was a screeching sound sometimes sounding like an old metal pub sign swinging in the wind. On the west side of the island, one of the man-made caves could be entered from the steep path down to Copper cove. The tunnel is about ten yards long and ends in a short cul-de-sac. Water seeps through the rocks and collects in a hollow, and when this was the only source of drinking water on the island, it had to be carried laboriously up the steep path from the cave across to the cottage. A small earth tremor cracked the cave floor and in our time only a small pool remained, which would not have been sufficient for us, and certainly not enough for the McWilliam family and their animals, who were the tenants before Mr. Houston.

The twenty five inch map of the island shows that a well was sunk on the ledge of rock above the beach where the cottage is situated, but there is no trace of that well now. The well on the shore that was now in use, had been dug by the lighthouse engineers. Later, a pipe had been fitted from the well up to the cottage into a tank in the kitchen. It was hard work pumping the water up to the cottage, and this made us very careful, never wasting water. Over forty years later, I am still very careful with water. Although I am polite and never chide my guests, I hate it when they fill the electric kettle to the brim and use electricity to boil it just for two cups of tea. Not only is water wasted, but also precious fuel. To save pumping up water from the well, we used rain water for washing and all household chores. A very large water tank, just outside the kitchen door, caught the rain water from the roof of the cottage. We were grateful for the large water butt as we needed a lot of water for cleaning, when we were at last able to enter the cottage after it had been thoroughly fumigated.

The cottage had not been decorated for thirty years, and had been badly neglected for the previous ten years. So before we moved in it had to be thoroughly cleaned and completely redecorated. Our first job was to clear out the byres so that we could use them to live in for a few weeks. There had been no animals kept on the island for many years, so the task was not too difficult. The beautiful sunny weather continued which made our temporary living quarters quite enjoyable, for we spent the time when we were not working, outside enjoying the panoramic views of cloudless skies and blue rippled seas with the wonderful backdrop of Screel and Bengairn. We never ceased to be captivated by the changing colours of these hills, as hour by hour their beauty changed as the clouds and sun moved across the sky. The evenings were indescribably beautiful as the sun set behind the hills and the golden colours of the sunset were reflected in the mud flats at low tide.

We stripped off the old wall paper and to our delight discovered some of the history of the cottage. Before papering the sitting room walls, the date of decoration had been recorded together with the names of the family. The previous tenants to Mr. Houston, the McWilliams, had moved to the island in 1927, when they decorated the walls. They had a child and named her May Maxwell, after the heroine in Crockett's book, which was based on Heston Island. S. R. Crockett was a Galloway writer who wrote Scots kailyard love novels, and he died in 1914. "The Raiders" was an action packed adventure set on Heston, named Rathan Isle in the story. The hero inherits the island and woos his roguish sweetheart, May Maxwell, who lives on the Mainland. The story involves smugglers, cut-throats, chases through the wild hills of the Glenkens, and descriptions of the spacious cave at the south of the island. At a very low tide it is possible to scramble down the cliffs at the south end of Heston and enter this famous cave. As a break from the back aching tasks of cleaning the cottage and clearing the sheds, we decided to explore the large cave. When we entered we were greeted by a number of rock pigeons we had disturbed, who flew out just above our heads, frightening the life out of us. The cave is smaller than that described in the novel, and the author had used much imagination in transforming the damp dark cave into a palatial home and hiding place for our pursued hero.

We spent many weeks transforming our island cottage and it was very hard work. When we were married our first terraced house was dark, all the paint work brown and gloomy. To counteract this our first new house had wood work painted in pure white with ivory walls. We loved the uncluttered lightness of our new home, but by the time we moved to Scotland, we were growing tired of the antiseptic cold look of all the rooms. Again we compensated for this by buying paint which could be coloured, and we picked out the woodwork in blues, yellows and pinks, and we pasted up colourful wall paper. Years later when we went back to visit the island, we were astounded at the colour schemes, and wondered how we could ever have enjoyed living in such an inartistic surrounding. The floor of the living room was made of sandstone slabs which were rough and uneven and had had no covering over them. It seems that they had not been cleaned for at least ten years, and it took a whole bucket of soapy water to clean each square yard. We used the water from the rainwater tank which although of a large capacity was getting dangerously low. We could heat water on our new calor gas cooker, but to save fuel we also used the old boiler in the kitchen which we fuelled with drift wood washed up on the shore.

There was no bathroom, but we had plans to convert the corrugated porch which sheltered the front door. It was divided into two small compartments. Our first job was to clear out all the rubbish that was stored there, for Mr. Houston had used the space as a junk room. The old man spent much of his time reading westerns and one of the compartments was stacked with old paper backs. Amongst these we found an ancient set of Encyclopaedia Brittanica. At that time, the present craze for buying anything old was not in vogue. We saved some of the books that were in better condition and enjoyed reading them in the winter months. The Encyclopaedia were old and out of date and so they were put out along with hundreds of tatty paperbacks. We lugged them down to the shore and had a spectacular bonfire. A few weeks later one of the fishermen asked if we had kept the Encyclopaedia as someone in the Anchor Hotel had shown interest in them, and was willing to buy them, but alas, it was too late, and we missed out on making a bit of money. The other compartment of the porch was stacked with old milk tins. As already mentioned, Mr. Houston had saved them, thinking that one day he would solder up all the holes he had pierced in them, and use them to make buoyancy tanks for his old boat. Fortunately, he never achieved this ambition, for besides the hours of work that would have been required, they would soon have disintegrated from rust once the salt water had splashed over them. We managed to clear these by loading them into weighted sacks, and dropping them into deep water in one of the crevices in the cliffs. Having cleared and cleaned out the porch we used the half by the door as an entrance and the inner half became our bathroom.

Below the cottage on the shore was an ancient bath that had been used as a water trough in the days when the McWilliams kept a few cows. We inspected the bath, it was very rusty but was not damaged and seemed to hold water all right. We felt sure that we could de-rust it and paint it, but the problem was hauling it up the fifty feet of steep path to the cottage. The only way was brute force, so John and I heaved and levered it up bit by bit. It was very hard, painful work, but we were determined that it would grace our new bathroom, and we finally accomplished our aim. The rust was chipped off and the bath dragged into the inner porch where a a drain pipe was fitted to it so that the water could drain away. There was no running water, all the water was carried through in buckets from the boiler which was filled from the rain tank. Before this could happen it was painted; this was a slow job as it needed three coats of thick lead paint, and it needed a fortnight to dry between each coat. John finished it off with two coats of heat-resistant white enamel. While all this was happening we had our bath in the boiler in the kitchen. After heating the water we had to remove all the hot drift wood and allow the bottom of the boiler to cool down before we could climb in and conduct our ablutions. Since the boiler was on the side of the kitchen where the sloping corrugated roof was quite low, bathing was a dif-ficult process, and sometimes painful if we came into contact with parts of the boiler that had not cooled down sufficiently. You can see why we were so keen on having a proper bath.

The first bath was quite an occasion, especially as we worried about the durability of the paint. As we poured bucket after bucket of steaming water into our new bath, we watched carefully to see if the paint would lift. It didn't feel sticky, so John gallantly climbed in and gently lowered himself on to the gleaming paint. All was well, he didn't stick to the bottom, and except for the hard work of carrying the water through, we enjoyed using our bath. We had brought with us a wash hand basin bought for a pound from a demolished theatre in Birmingham. This was fitted with a drainage pipe, and our bathroom was almost complete. Mr. Houston used an old wooden shed behind the cottage for toilet purposes, but we intended to have the facility of an indoor toilet. There was no way that we could fit a flushed toilet and we made do with quite a good looking chemical toilet. We were very pleased when eventually our bathroom was complete and in use.

While all this hard work was proceeding we still needed to attend to our lighthouse duties. It was a minor light built about a hundred years before our tenancy. In those days the Solway was busy with shipping, and Palnackie, the village above Kippford on the River Urr, was a busy port. The town of Dalbeattie was also a port with more than half a dozen schooners tied alongside at one time. It must have been quite difficult sailing up the river as the river winds for miles before reaching the town. Heston seems to have been uninhabited at this time and the lighthouse was built to guide the shipping, and the old cottage was rebuilt to house someone to look after the lighthouse. If the well was sunk at that time, it must have been updated later, since the equipment was not old. The amazing thing about the well was that it was situated only a few feet from the high tide line. At high tide the level of the water in the well was below sea level, yet there was no trace of saltiness in the water.

The lighthouse was built at the top of the cliffs at the south-east corner of the island where the deep channel from the Solway swings up the east side of Heston. Although only a small light it can be seen from all over the Solway and from Palnackie and the Rough Firth between Kippford and Rockcliffe. If we spent the weekend away from Heston there were several points on the mainland where we could check that the light was still working. We also needed to make sure that its flashing sequence was correct, for it was by this that shipping knew which light they were observing. Later, we bought a small cottage in Dalbeattie where we could spend the night when we were off the island, and a good viewing point for the light was at a high point in the cemetery beyond the Rounall Woods.

When we visited the island in April the gas used to fuel the lighthouse was acetylene and it was produced by dripping water on to carbide. I remember my father telling me that in his early days of cycling the lamps on the bicycle worked on the same principle. By the time we came to live on Heston, the light-house engineers had altered the mechanism of the light, ready for our taking over its upkeep. The new system was much more reliable. It was still fuelled by acetylene, but the messy production method had been changed. The gas now came in large cylinders, and the acetylene gas could not be compressed like the calor gas we used for our cooker, but was stored in acetone. This made the cylinders very heavy, even when all the gas was used up. The fishermen were paid to transport the cylinders to the island and four were needed, weighing about two hundredweight's each. A trolley had been provided for us to transport the cylinders from the shore up to the lighthouse, and since the way up was very steep, a lot of effort and energy was required to drag and push the heavy trolley up grassy paths.

The residue of lime from the old system was used to white wash the lighthouse building, and once a year inspectors arrived from the Northern Lights Commission. All lighthouses guide shipping and protect ships from going aground. The major lighthouses round the coast, at that time, had resident keepers to manually take care of the lighthouses, but the minor lights were automatic and did not need constant supervision. However, the light still needed to be checked daily, kept painted and neat, with the lantern constantly cleaned, as the salt spray soon dimmed the light. There were two rooms in the lighthouse one housing all the paint and cleaning equipment, and the other where the mechanism and the gas cylinders were kept. We were responsible for looking after the system, and weighing the cylinders so that they could be replaced before the gas ran out. The lantern was on the roof and reached by a ladder. On days when a gale was blowing the ladder had to be securely tied to the lighthouse. The lenses were protected by glass panels that could be opened to reach the light when the lenses were cleaned, and to re-light the lantern. The Northern Light Commissioners had our light system on trial. Since the bottled acetylene presented many problems in handling, especially as the gas was dangerously explosive, they discarded this means of fuelling the minor lights and later replaced the gas with propane. The installation of the new system involved our boarding the engineers, and was a very interesting two weeks, the story of which will be told later.

Along with the tasks of preparing the cottage for habitation, clearing the byres for John's organ building, and looking after the lighthouse, we needed to gather as much home grown food as possible, so when we moved on to the island we were anxious to discover how our two walled gardens had fared. The garden planted with potatoes did not look very healthy. However, the patch of rhubarb had benefited from the seaweed compost and we were soon able to pull rhubarb. The carrots, lettuce, onions and radishes were coming along well. Presently, there is much concern about the advisability of using genetically modified foods. This has reminded me of experiments that John did when we first moved on to Heston. As he was a scientist and worked in research, he was able to irradiate some of the seeds that we planted, so that he could see if it helped or hindered their growth and production of food. Sadly nothing happened, the irradiated seeds grew and were no different from the ordinary seeds. We decided that we would grow tomatoes and a good place between two old buildings seemed a good location. A frame work from sturdy wooden poles, which we had found near the shore, was constructed at the side of one of the byres, sheltered by the cliff to the rear. This was covered with heavy-duty polythene, which we had brought with us for that purpose. The polythene was very thick and we secured it well, for we knew that there would be gales. We then needed to buy the tomato plants and this we did as soon as we were able to make our way independently to and from the island.

One of the newspaper reporters was brought over by the salmon fisherman, Eddie, from Balcary, and through this encounter with Eddie we found another way of getting on and off the island. Until then all our mainland contacts had been via Kippford. We had not attempted to try to walk off the island, having been strongly warned by Mr. Houston never to try because of the quick sands. It was a four mile tortuous boat journey to Kippford, and it would be good if we could use Balcary, which was much nearer, especially if it were possible to walk off. At low tide the sea receded leaving a large expanse of mud flats which connected the island right across to the bay at Balcary. We could see a hotel on the bay, and we knew that the village of Auchencairn was probably less than a mile from Balcary, and no doubt had a village shop like Kippford. Until now, we had bought our messages from Kippford, and the mussel men brought over our order. For the first few weeks, until we were independent with our own dinghy, we relied upon them. They were out most days musselling and we always came down to them and made them a pot of tea. They also had a contract with the Post Office to deliver our mail. Our grocery order was usually correct but there were occasions when items, such as bread were forgotten. On one occasion we were off the island and called at the shop to pay our bill, pointing out that we had not received the loaves ordered. We discovered that the loaves had been given to the fishermen. It was a week after the grocery delivery and we found the loaves still sitting on the sea wall!

Eddie was asked if it were possible to walk from the island to Balcary. The answer was yes, it was possible, but caution needed to be exercised. He had learned the correct way over as a boy walking to the island with his grandfather. It was possible to avoid the quick sands if you kept high up on the flats, aiming first of all for the Almorness Point headland. The snag was that there was the Orchardton Lane to cross which could be difficult. A lane, in Galloway, is a water that drains marshy ground, and this lane drained the merse at the head of the Balcary Bay. It was a small river that could be quite shallow at times, and at others a rushing torrent. The River Urr runs along the east side of Almorness Point and Orchardton Lane on the west side. Heston lies between the two rivers. The east side dries out at low tide as well as the west, but the River Urr is too deep to cross on foot. As a young boy Eddie was told always to take a stick when crossing the lane and feel ahead with the stick before taking a step. Like many young people, he thought he knew best. He looked at the lane, which appeared to be shallow, and decided that a stick might be advisable for an old man, but he did not need one. Half way across he was suddenly up to his waist in water with his legs trapped and bruised, a hole had been scoured out by the stones shifting in the strong current. The firm sands are suitable for walking over, but under the hard layer is clayey mud. The current in the lane causes stones in the bed to gouge out grooves and often these grooves deepen making gutters and holes which can be quite deep. The stick is to feel for these gutters and avoid them. It was good that we had met up with Eddie for we became friends, and following his advice we discovered a better means of access to Heston. Not only could we walk off if the weather and tides were suitable, but we also used that crossing in our dinghy. We had to allow for the current, according to the tide, but the crossing was much shorter.

Eddie also gave us the use of one of his fish houses, where we could keep our wee car. From then on, we bought our groceries from the Auchencairn store and called, on our return to the island, at the Seaside farm for milk. It was lovely drinking fresh milk again, we had not enjoyed the tinned variety very much. The farmer's wife filled our billycan from the milk churn, and it was usually fifty percent cream. We thoroughly enjoyed our new found freedom by the Balcary route.

The fact that we could more easily travel off the island, enabled John to offi-cially take on the post of organist for the churches at Colvend and Southwick. As soon as we had the independence of our dinghy John started to play the organ, but we could not always guarantee that the weather would be suitable for us to motor over to Rockcliffe every Sunday. The minister's wife played when we were unable to attend, but found it inconvenient, as she had other duties and a family to look after. The church at Southwick was a beautiful wee church, but was many miles away along the coast and heughs, and it meant that lunch was always late on Sunday's. When we needed to rely on our boat, our trips off the island depended on the tide, but also on the weather. Now we had the choice of using the boat to take us to Rockcliffe or walking off at low tide when the sea was too wild for us. It was a good few miles round to Colvend in the Bond-Mini, but it enabled us to be regular at church. All our lives we had enjoyed joining with others in fellowship and worship, so we were delighted that we could now continue regular church attendance. The eighty pounds a year organist's fee, increased our income by over fifty percent, a hundred pounds coming from looking after the lighthouse and wintering sheep. Our lives became governed by the tide and we have been known, on many occasions, to leave or come on to Heston in the middle of the night when the state of the tides required this. There usually seemed to be sufficient light from the afterglow, or moon to show us the silhouette of Almorness Point, and we learned to line up the hills to give us the right direction for crossing the lane.

Because of the articles which appeared in the press, we received a letter one day from the BBC asking us if we would record an interview for their countryside programme. An arrangement was made for us to motor over to Balcary to meet the interviewer, where we talked, answering his questions and giving our views of island life. The recording was made as we sat on the rocks by the fish house, and Eddie motored around the bay to give a suitable background noise. At the end of the session we were very surprised to be given two pounds. This was a great improvement on the newspaper reports, for which we received nothing, not even copies of the photographs they had taken, and promised to send us. The date and time when the broadcast would be made was noted, and we were anxious to listen to it. As it was a lunch time Sunday programme, that day we took our portable radio with us in the boat. Our picnic was eaten sitting in the boat as she lay on the sandy beach, and we waited for the programme anxious to hear what we sounded like. I think that was the first time that we had ever heard our recorded voices and it was a strange experience. There were a number of people talking on the programme and we listened carefully for our voices. I recognised John's voice and he mine, but neither of us recognised our own voices. Even now when I have forgotten to switch off the answering machine and hear my own voice answering a call, I am still surprised that it is really me speaking.

Chapter 5 **Sea and Gales.**

"More majestic than the thunders of mighty waters, more majestic than the waves of the sea, majestic on high is the Lord." (Psalm 93 v 4.)

There was a great deal of hard work to be done before we could move into our new home, cleaning, painting and decorating the cottage took quite a while. We also had the lighthouse duties and the garden to tend. John also needed to get on with making the rather decrepit, large byre suitable as a workshop, so that he could start to build pipe organs. After we had settled into island life we became more confident in using the boat, and soon learned that we must carry our dinghy up to the top of the shell and pebble beach, out of the way of the sea. It was hard work and needed both of us to lift it. The outer hull could easily be holed by dragging it over the rough stones and shells. We had wondered if we could construct rails down the steep part of the beach to winch the boat into safety, and lessen the hard work. This idea was soon abandoned as the shape of the beach continually altered. After a storm and high seas the contours of the beach bore no resemblance to those of the previous day. Water is very powerful and as we stood watching we could hear the pebbles rattling down the steep slope of shingle as the tide receded and sucked the shells and stones, remoulding the shape of the beach.

When the sea was relatively calm, we carried the dinghy down onto the sea, and began to explore the south side of the island which was always surrounded by water. The bays around the Almorness Point were explored, by boat when the tide was high, and on foot at low tide. The shell beach jutted out at the north side of the island leading into the large, barnacled rocks which became smaller and formed the spine of the rack This stretched to within two hundred yards of the Almorness point, and the remaining area was firm sand. To the west side of the rack, at low tide, there were two pools, and the fishermen often anchored their boat in one of the pools. The firm sands, always covered with a layer of water, stretched out either side of the rack, Balcary to the west, and the River Urr on the east side. It was lovely walking bare foot over the wet sands, but I could never get used to walking over the rack with bare feet, it was far too painful. John's feet hardened and he rarely took an old pair of shoes with him for the rocky, mussel covered rack.

Copper Cove was a good place to bathe, and gave us a time of relaxation from the heavy work. Neither of us were good swimmers, but we enjoyed messing about in the water when the weather was warm. We quickly learned to respect the sea, for it could be treacherous. When there was a storm out at sea, we were warned by the big swell which came rolling in round the south end of the island. The seas surged along the east channel at the north end of Heston and white crests would begin to develop. However, it took more experience than we possessed to know whether the swell was heralding a storm or was the tail end of a storm out at sea. One Sunday we were about to set off for Rockcliffe and we noticed that there was a swell, but the waves were not topped with white crests and we decided it would be all right to make our way across to the mainland. Usually it took some hours before a big storm developed and we would be back home well in time. The trip across was easy and as we came into Rockcliffe bay, John switched off the motor and turned to lift the outboard onto its bracket before we grounded on the beach. Just at that moment a breaker came rushing up the bay and broke as it came up to the boat drenching the boat and John in the stern. The boat was hauled well above the high tide mark and we turned to watch quite spectacular waves breaking on the shore. Hopefully, by the time we had been to church and had our lunch, the sea would be calmer and we would be able to get off the beach safely.

An enjoyable afternoon was spent at the manse as we waited for the tide to turn and the sea to come up into Rockcliffe bay ready for us to launch the boat and make our way home. Elsie Jack, the minister's wife, had offered us a bed for the night if the weather became too bad for us to venture home in our wee dinghy. We walked down to the bay about teatime and the sea was covering the sands, and there was soon enough water for us to push the boat into the sea and lower the motor. The sea was calm and very little wind, and we decided that it was safe for us to set out to the island. The breakers of the morning must have been the remnants of an earlier storm out at sea. The first part of our journey was well sheltered by Rough Island. As we came out of the shelter of the island a swell started to build up from the south-west but we were not worried we had been out in far bigger swells. The swell continued to increase and as we came out of the shelter of the Almorness peninsular we were hit by a strong wind, which must have been a force 6 gale. As the wind from the north-west came into contact with the souwesterly swell the water began to churn and the waves built up, crested with white foam. We were over half way home, and decided that it was not worth turning back. The driven spray stung our eyes and made it difficult to see. The currents also made it very difficult to steer the boat in the right direction. I was sitting in the bow and receiving the full force of the waves as they battered the boat. The breakers were coming from different directions and it was impossible to steer towards our landing place, and we were heading towards the cliffs. My worry was that one of the waves would swamp the motor and John would be unable to start it again; it certainly would have been impossible to row the boat ashore in those seas. John's consoling words were that the currents would probably sweep us back up the estuary and we would make the mainland safely. There was no worry about the boat sinking, for the double hull housed buoyancy tanks. We also always wore life jackets when we were at sea, which were ex RAF inflatable jackets, well proven.

As we came nearer to the island we could see the Solway Yacht Club outer buoy which marked the outer most point for the yacht races. The base is a strong steel construction, topped by a six foot flag pole. Much to our horror we could see this hefty buoy being tossed around by the tumultuous waves with both buoy and flagpole regularly disappearing beneath the waves. The wind had pushed us off course and we were heading for the wrong side of the buoy, and the currents made it impossible to head for the shore, but were sweeping us towards the nastiest part of the Heston cliffs. The only comfort was that once we were under the cliffs we would be sheltered from the gale. Thank God the motor was not swamped and, after what seemed like an eternity, we reached the shelter of Heston's cliffs. In the lee of the cliffs we were able to make our way cautiously, avoiding the rock outcrops, and reached our landing place safely. We hauled the boat up on to the top of the pebbly beach, and stood dripping wet watching the stretch of white, tumbling water which separated us from Rockcliffe. We had made it! We were thankful for our safe return home, and I am sure that John also felt a glow of pride that we had managed to conquer those vicious seas in our fourteen foot dinghy.

The storm caused us trouble in our food production. During the night the gale increased and we woke the next morning to find our heavy duty polythene greenhouse shredded, the plastic remains flapping woefully, hanging in ribbons from the sturdy framework. Even the tomato plants were in a pitiful state and those we were able to salvage were placed behind the cottage where there was a little shelter from the cliff rising above it. Most of these eventually died, the few that survived producing marble sized tomatoes. As it happened we discovered that the soil we had used for the tomatoes was infected and we would never have harvested a good crop of tomatoes anyway. The walled garden of potatoes yielded less potatoes by weight than those we had planted. The Ministry of Agriculture and Fisheries were contacted to give us their advice. One day Eddie brought a man from the department of agriculture over in his boat, and he looked at our land and told us that the soil in the two walled gardens was infected with eel worm which had attacked the potato tubers.

This disease was caused through the land being used repeatedly to grow the same crop. In the past this must have happened on Heston. There are signs of 'lazy beds' on Heston. These are ridges of turf cut out along the hill slope with the potatoes planted along the turf beds, fertilised with seaweed. If the potatoes were grown on the same beds year in year out, this could have caused the infection. It could be that the whole of the island was infected with the eel worm. Heston had good deep soil and at one time it was very successfully farmed, producing good crops, as well as grassland for animals. In our dream planning for Heston we were hoping to invest in some machinery to plough up part of the land to grow crops, and perhaps also keep live stock. In our tenancy contract, there was a clause that we could only dig up half an acre of land, so we did not attempt to cultivate any other land except for the two walled gardens. Tomatoes belong to the same family as potatoes, so our plants would never have flourished and provided a crop for us. The advise we were given was to refrain from planting potatoes for at least seven years. Thinking about it now, I wonder how this would have cured the problem, for I feel sure that Mr. Houston had not planted potatoes on the land, and his tenancy had lasted for ten years, so it had already lain fallow for well over the seven years. I suppose there was a possibility that he had planted potatoes in his early years, and the eel worm infestation had not had time to clear.

The storms did not damage the rhubarb, carrots or lettuce and we made the most of these crops. There were a lot of rats on Heston and they developed a liking for carrots. Fortunately, the carrots flourished on the seaweed manured land, and even after the rats has gnawed off the top two inches, there was plenty left for us. The lettuce also benefited from the seaweed, and grew to a tremendous size, some of them weighing three pounds. Unfortunately, they all matured at the same time and we grew tired of eating lettuce with every meal. I even tried cooking it as a vegetable, but the result was a soggy mess, so we stuck to eating it fresh. We were doing our best to live off the land as much as possible, so I did not want to waste any of the food. We have, on several occasions eaten rhubarb and lettuce for breakfast!

That first year the sea also was a source of food for us. I have recounted the disaster of fishing from the dinghy, but Jeff introduced us to another way of catching fish. A line was stretched between two poles and dangling from it were half a dozen small cords each ending in a fish hook. These were baited with fresh mussels. This was a messy business, prying open the mussel shell and impaling the contents onto the hook. The line was stretched out at the edge of the sea, near to the mussel covered rack, and the hooks baited as the tide was coming up. The theory was that the fish would make for the rack to eat the mussels, and be attracted by a free meal dangling just above the mud flats, near by. I was surprised that fish could feed off the hard shelled mussels, but evidently their strong teeth enable them to open the mussel shells to secure the soft mussel body. Mussels already shelled would be a great temptation. This bait was also attractive to the gulls and it was necessary to bait the hooks at the last minute so that the tide would safely cover them. As the tide comes in quickly it was work that had to be done fast. The most important bit was to be there to harvest the fish at the right time, just as the tide receded and the water left the line. Our island was a great sanctuary for many birds, but mostly seagulls, especially heron gulls and great black backed gulls. They were always ready for a free meal and we needed to reach the line before they did. We could not control the time of the tides, and it meant sometimes getting up as soon as it was light to rescue the fish, in the summer as early as three o'clock. The gulls did not feed in the dark so the hours of darkness were uninterrupted. Codling were caught and we thoroughly enjoyed eating fresh fish, although gutting and cleaning the fish was not a pleasant occupation. Fish bought from a shop tastes very different from that caught freshly from the sea. On the occasions when we visited our parents, who still lived in the Midlands, John's mother always cooked haddock for tea on the day we arrived. We ate it out of politeness, but we certainly did not enjoy it. It was a long time after our fishing days, before I ever bought fish from a shop.

After we came to know Eddie, we had another source of fish. Eddie was a salmon fisher, and fished with fixed nets. He had two sets of nets running from the shore which ended in pockets. The nets were fixed on poles and were tall and strong. As the tide came up the fish swam into the net and to escape followed the net down into the deeper water and were caught in the pockets. Eddie sold the fish to hoteliers in Dumfries. Salmon were not the only fish to be caught in the nets, there were often sand dabs there too, a tasty small flat fish. During the permitted salmon fishing season, we were often given half a dozen flat fish, to carry back to Heston. They were a lovely sweet fish and we liked them more than the codling. The salmon fishing season was restricted, and the pockets must be opened on Sundays, so that the fish could not be caught on the Sabbath.

The weekend was sometimes spent on the mainland, and we always checked the lighthouse from one of the vantage points. One weekend while we were off, a storm blew up, and we walked down to the shore at Rockcliffe to check the light. Much to our frustration we could not see the light flashing. After watching for awhile in case a squall had blotted out the light from our view, it was still not visible. The outline of Heston could be seen like a dark shadow, but no flashes from the lighthouse, so we feared the worst, the light had blown out. There was a gale blowing, and we knew that there was no way that we could reach the island in our dinghy. Our only hope was to ask Eddie if he would take us across in his much larger boat. He was not on the phone, so we left a message with his neighbour, the district nurse, that we were on our way round. Eddie was proud of the sea worthiness of his boat and was known to be reckless, so we believed that he would take us. Eddie was picked up in our van and as we were leaving we heard his wife shouting at him not to take his boat out in the storm. I think that clinched it. Have you noticed that opposition to a project strengthens your determination to go ahead? He called out to her "Dinna call out the life boat, woman, or I'll divorce ye." One look at the sea made it certain that we could never have crossed over in our small dinghy. We could hear the roar of the breakers coming into the bay, but we seemed to be partly sheltered from the gale. Eddie's voice was snatched away by the gale as he called to us "We'll try it, if it gets too bad, we'll have to turn back." The boat was moored in Balcary Bay in front of the Hotel, but his dinghy was tied up at the end of the salmon nets where he had been working, and was cut off from the land by the sea. The hotel proprietor, Tom, who was the local Shipwrecked Mariner's representative, came to our aid and lent us his dinghy to row Eddie out to his boat. Eddie rowed out with John, who then returned the dinghy to the shore, while Eddie started the motor and collected his own dinghy. This was necessary as the hotel dinghy had been vandalised by some holiday makers and leaked like a sieve. Fortunately, it was not far to Eddie's boat and John stuffed some rag into the biggest hole and then bailed out the leaking dinghy with his shoe, the only thing to hand, while Eddie rowed. They tipped the water out of the boat before John returned, rowing as fast as he could to get back before the dinghy sank.

Tom volunteered to come with us, and the three of us were collected and boarded the bigger boat. It was good that Tom had come with us for he was needed to row us ashore at Heston. By this time it was almost midnight and quite dark. I was glad of this, for at least we could not see the menacing waves which began to tower towards us threatening to bury us under their mass. In the daylight the whole chaotic waste of tumbling water would have been even more frightening. As each wave approached the crest was faintly phosphorescent and this enabled Eddie to swing the boat and take it on the bow. The shape of the island loomed up looking menacing in the darkness, and we dropped anchor in the lee of the point. It would have been much too dangerous to take the boat near the cliffs. The fishing boat was catching much of the force of the gale and the anchor was not holding, so Eddie needed to stay with his boat to keep the engine running and prevent the boat from drifting to the shore. The rocks on the shore would have torn the bottom out of the hull. Tom was going to row us ashore; at least Eddie's dinghy was a strong fisherman's vessel. The dinghy was brought round to the side and as the fishing boat rose and sank on the waves the wee boat cavorted like a mad thing. Tom and John held the dinghy as firmly as they could while I was pushed over the side before I could argue about going first. They both jumped in after me and pushed off from the boat and rowed towards the point of the island which was a mass of foaming water. We could not risk driving the dinghy ashore for strong as it was it would have smashed against the stones. John and I jumped out of the boat, waist deep in water, and pushed the dinghy off as far as we could. Tom needed to row back as quickly as possible to help Eddie haul up the anchor, for the boat had the full force of the gale battering against it.

I ran up to the cottage and hastily lit the hurricane lamp, and carried it down to the shore to show Eddie exactly where the point of the island and the rocks were. He needed to clear the point and quickly steer away from the dangerous rocks. We faintly heard Eddie's voice in the darkness shouting that he was clear. The return journey would be just as hazardous, with no lights from the farms or hotel to guide them back, for it was well after midnight. I stayed on the shore with the lamp waiting for a signal from Eddie that he had made it safely, while John climbed up the hill with all the equipment he would need to re-light the lantern. When a gale was blowing, lighting the lamp was a difficult task and it was essential to take ropes and anchor yourself to the light to prevent being blown over the cliffs, while both hands were being used to rekindle the light. Down on the shore eventually I saw a dim light as Eddie flashed his torch to signal their safe arrival. I thanked God as I trudged up to the cottage, and breathed a sigh of relief that the dangerous journey had ended well, with no casualties from the night's adventure. We were exhausted and drenched to the skin, but thankful to be home with the prospects of a good night's sleep.

These skirmishes with the sea gave us a healthy respect for it, and we tried never to take chances with the sea. Those first two months on Heston were hard work, with much to learn about the sea and island life, but we thoroughly enjoyed ourselves, and revelled in the freedom of living alone and enjoying the surrounding beauty. After a hard day, or an exciting adventure, it was good to sit up on the cliffs and relax, as we watched the yachts cutting through the water to round the Heston buoy as they raced back to Kippford. Bigger yachts with colourful sails and spinnakers ballooning in the wind often passed behind the island. Always there were gulls wheeling through the sky, their calls to be heard from early morning till late at night. We never grew tired of enjoying the beauty and power of God's wonderful creation, and gave thanks to him for it.

Chapter 6 **Household Stores.**

"She is like the merchant ships, bringing her food from afar. She gets up while it is still dark; she provides food for her family." Proverbs. ch. 31 vv 14 and 15.

We had now settled into using Balcary as our mainland base. Our Bond-Mini was kept in the fish house, and when we needed to shop we chose a good day and motored over and then picked up the car to drive the mile into Auchencairn. By this time I was well used to my calor gas cooker, and decided that in future I would make my own bread. There had already been problems with the delivery of bread. Sometimes it came into the Kippford shop late, and on one occasion, as already recounted, the mussel men had left it on the sea wall where we found it the next time we were over to Kippford. John also loved cakes, so a cake baking session was also a must, although we did enjoy some lovely cakes bought at the bakers in Castle Douglas. Our favourites were pineapple creams and jap cakes. The latter were wonderful gooey cakes with a creamy filling, covered with chocolate and rolled in nuts. Many years later, when visiting the area, I bought these particular cakes. I was very disappointed for they did not taste at all the same. As with many things, the imagination of past joys is far better than the reality.

It made sense to buy our stores in large quantities. When I looked through my telescope at the Cumberland coast, on a clear day I could see the Carr's flour mills, which were situated at Silloth. In those days the owner, Mr. Carr, was a regular visitor to Kippford where he sailed his yacht. He stayed at the house of one of the fishermen many weekends, and he agreed that we could purchase flour from the mill. It was to be delivered to the Auchencairn store, and we also ordered a sack of sugar. I hardly use sugar these days, but then I think we consumed as much sugar as other products. Eddie came by the island one day and shouted to us that our flour was in stock. When the weather and tides were suitable we left the island and picked up our two sacks of flour from the shop. They were quite heavy and difficult to load into the car. They would not fit into the boot, so we loaded them onto the passenger seat, and I perched on the back of the car for the short journey to the fish house. They were then manhandled into the boat and carried up the hill to the cottage. By this time we had our wheelbarrow to help carry heavy goods from the shore to the cottage. We stowed the two sacks of flour into the pantry, a small room off the kitchen. I was anxious to try my hand at baking again, having been used to baking my own bread before we moved to Scotland. However, it had to wait as I had forgotten to buy a tin of dried yeast, and in any case we still had some shop bread left, and there was still much cleaning work to be done.

A few days later, Eddie came across and had an important message for us from the shop. The gist of his conversation, shouted across the water from his boat, was that we must not use the flour. It seemed that the flour mill in Carlisle had sent us flour that was unsuitable for human consumption, and we must return it. I was glad that I had been forced to put off my baking, and thought that the flour must be contaminated in some way and could have made us ill. At the next suitable tide we loaded up the flour, landed at the fish house, and again struggled to get the flour into the car, and returned it to the shop. Apparently, this flour which was unfit for human consumption, was flour destined for a fish and chip shop. It was flour used to batter the fish! I wonder what regular fish and chip eaters would have made of the message "Unfit for human consumption" We had to wait a few more days until the good flour was delivered. On arrival at the shop to collect our flour, we found the shop full of customers all waiting to be served. "The flour's in the back room under the table", we were told. "Would you mind helping yourself." This we duly did, locating a table with two sacks of flour, and heaving it outside and once again into the Bond-Mini. John had just started the engine ready to drive off, when the shopkeeper came rushing out of the shop waving his arms. There were two tables in the back room, each with two sacks of flour beneath. Two were the old sacks waiting to be returned to Carlisle, and the other two waiting for us. Of course, we had loaded the wrong sacks onto the car! Yet again the sacks were hauled off the Bond, and replaced with the new sacks, the flour suitable for human consumption!

There was a sad postscript to this story. A number of weeks later returning to the island we found the cottage covered with black footprints. The rats, which inhabited the island, had broken into the cottage. They had entered through the boiler flue, hence the sooty foot marks. You can guess which food they had made for. Yes, the sacks of flour. They had attacked both sacks and created a tremendous mess. Rats are well known as disease carriers, and we did not fancy using the flour after they had gnawed through the sacks and helped themselves. We threw the flour away, and after that bought the flour in smaller quantities and kept it in a large tin. The rats found their way into the cottage, but could not find their way out again through the flue. Instead they gnawed their way through the kitchen door which was made of really thick wood. The bottom of the door was repaired with metal sheets, to make sure that the rats could not enter that way. We had no further trouble with the rats entering the cottage, although we still shared our carrots with them. There were a lot of rats around the cottage and we set traps for them, but they were very cunning and always seemed to manage to get at the bait without setting off the trap. When we were shopping we bought some large cage traps, baited them and weighted them down with rocks. The next morning we discovered that the bait had gone. The rats had burrowed underneath and extracted the food through the bars on the underside of the trap. After we left Heston, the rats became very numerous, and on one occasion when Eddie had landed on the island in the dark, he heard a rustling noise around his feet and discovered that he was surrounded by a large number of rats. After this experience he tried to gas the rats with cyanide, but was not very successful.

At first we used tinned milk, which I certainly did not like, and it was good to bring back a billycan of fresh, creamy milk from the farm whenever we were off the island. Later, we discovered a dried milk, which not only had the advantage of a long storage life, but also had the cream made from vegetable fat, so it was healthier for us. Most of our groceries were purchased from the shop in Auchencairn, although we occasionally drove into Castle Douglas for any special needs.

Most days Fred and Jeff from Kippford arrived to carry out their gruelling four hours of back breaking mussel picking. In the early weeks, before we discovered the advantages of using Balcary as our mainland port of call, they would bring over our groceries and post. Half way through their taxing work, I would take them a pot of tea, and they appreciated the break from being bent over, often in rain and wind, their fingers frozen and grazed from cutting the mussels from the barnacle covered rocks on the rack. We enjoyed the contact with the outside world, especially when all the summer visitors had returned home, and our only companions were the seagulls. It was a good time to catch up on all the news from Kippford and the surrounding district. Later on we would have the sheep for company. In spite, of being isolated we did not feel lonely. After the day's work was finished we enjoyed the solitude of Heston, and the comfort of our cottage, with plenty of books to read, a portable radio to listen to, and each other's company.

During that first summer we came to know the island well. The south end of the island was gull territory, mostly black backs, but we also had areas where the terns nested. It did not pay to get too near to their nests, if we did they came screaming at us, and their needle sharp beaks were to be avoided at all costs. During the breeding season it was advisable to go up to the light house armed with a stout stick, which could be waved over head to protect us from the dive bombing terns. Last time I was on the island, the gulls seemed to have taken over the north end of the island as well, but in my time they only nested at the south end. As well as the wrens and robins, blackbirds nested, and there was a pair of ravens in Copper Cove. I enjoyed watching the ringed plovers, a beautiful small bird that scurried along the pebble beach, or skimmed low over the water with its plaintive "Toooee, toooee, toooee" call. I found two chicks, which were so well camouflaged among the pebbles that they were difficult to see. The parents are very courageous birds, driving off the gulls and even once attacking an owl that came too near their nesting site. After we left Heston and there was no one living there, not only the rats became a nuisance, but also the gulls colonised the north of the island as well as the south. The result was that they cleared all the beautiful small birds from the island, the black birds, robins, wrens and pipits.

As I look out of my front window, I can see a wonderful patch of montbretia, its brilliant, orange flowers brightening up the garden. They always remind me of the montbretia growing on the cliffs at Heston. I do not know whether they were wild, or planted there, but together with the orange tiger lilies in the small garden around the cottage, they brighten up the island, even on the dullest day. There were other wild flowers growing in the crevices of the rocks, on the ledges, and on the hill side. The delicate Scottish bluebells, called hare bells in England, could be found together with heathers, bell heather and ling. There were patches of pink thrift growing on the cliffs, bird's foot trefoil and other common wild flowers. The brambles flowered, but I cannot remember ever picking any blackberries from them. I think the cold winds and salt spray, probably inhibited their growth.

Galloway is famous for its beautiful sunsets, which are reflected in the miles of wet mud flats. The holiday brochures call Galloway "The Land of Golden Sunsets". We had already treasured these wonders when we were on our camping holidays, but now we could sit by the window in the evening and watch the sun sink behind the mainland hills. It is impossible to capture the full glory of God's universe, whether in paintings or colour photographs. Those sunsets had to be experienced to know the joy of the light and colour bathing our amazing surroundings. The sky seemed to be tinted with a green background against which the golden red orb of the sun blazed. Wisps of clouds reflected the golden red, and as the sun sank behind the hills all the clouds were transformed by the suns reflected glory, and the whole scene was mirrored in the water covering the flats. Until I lived on Heston I had never realised how the immensity of the sky manifested the wonder of infinite space. That awareness of the awe and beauty of God's universe has never left me. Even today, passed my three score and ten years, I feel closest to God and can worship and adore him best of all, when I am out walking in the countryside, aware of the sky above and the vastness of creation. All the hard work, the uncertainty for the future, and the isolation was as nothing compared with the rewards of experiencing the glory of creation, exemplified by the beauty of the wonderful Galloway sunsets.

Chapter 7 **Visitors.**

"Be joyful in hope, patient in affliction, faithful in prayer. Share with God's people who are in need. Practice hospitality." (Romans chapter 12 vv 12 & 13.)

One of the reasons we drove ourselves so hard to make the cottage and surroundings presentable, was because we had invited our parents to come and stay with us for a holiday. We were determined that the cottage would be clean and bright and that there would be no traces of neglect to be seen. Our parents had questioned the wisdom of giving up good jobs to live miles away on an island, with no real income. I was resolved that they would, at least, see our new home in the very best light possible. However, those first couple of months were not one continual round of toil. The wonder and beauty of Heston had not been diminished by our hard work. It was early summer and it was good to sit on the cliffs and enjoy the peace, and stop and stare at our sun drenched island, at the ever changing sea, and the hills of the remote mainland. Although peaceful, Heston was not quiet. The gulls and terns uttered their plaintive calls, wrens popped in and out of the dry-stone wall, their lovely song amazing me in its loudness coming from such a tiny bird. Our resident robin definitely had a jealous streak. It was for ever furiously fighting its reflection in the kitchen window. The song of pipits accompanied me as I made my way through the bracken on the way to the lighthouse.

My parents arrived first. They had come by train from New Street station in Birmingham to Carlisle, and there caught the line to Dumfries and Dalbeattie. At this time the Dumfries to Dalbeattie line still existed and continued round the coast to Stranraer. Later, Mr. Beeching axed this line and it was necessary to collect our visitors from Dumfries. Now there is no sign of the Dalbeattie station or the large Creamery beside it, the whole area is a housing estate. We had some good sunny weather for their stay, but also rain and gales. By this time our house in England had been sold and we decided to buy a second-hand, small van. £500 of the money received from the sale was invested in one of the Scottish building societies. Our Bond-Mini was taken in part exchange for the van, and we were sad to lose our very first car, for we had had great adventures and fun in it. It was not suitable for our pipe organ business; we needed a vehicle with a carrying capacity, for it would be necessary to transport the equipment needed to build the organs, and to deliver the various components for installation in the church. With a view to carrying visitors, John fitted two removable seats in the back of the van. Collecting visitors from the station would have been impossible in the Bond-Mini. The tide was at the right state and they enjoyed the trip over to the island in our dinghy. I think that they were duly impressed with the beautiful scenery surrounding us. This was their first visit to Scotland, and Galloway is a wonderful introduction to the country. The highlands in the north-west of Scotland are well known and very impressive, and Galloway mirrors their beauty on a smaller scale.

The arrival of our first visitors gave us a chance to sit and relax. When the sun was shining, we sat in its warmth, making ourselves comfortable on the cliffs above the cottage, and watched the yachts slicing through the water, their sails billowing in the breeze. We delighted in seeing the seagulls skimming over the sea and soaring along the cliffs. The island was covered with lush grass, and encroaching bracken, but the thin soil on the cliff tops produced a profusion of wild flowers, purple thyme, yellow birds-foot trefoil, bluebells, thrift and campion. My parents enjoyed their stay with us, and we were able to take them in the van to explore parts of the region which were still new to us. One wonderful day out was spent driving to Castle Douglas and along Loch Ken, up to the village of New Galloway. Loch Ken became a huge stretch of water when the water level of all the lochs in this area was raised. The lochs were fed by the river Dee which flows out to the sea at Kirkcudbright. The water was needed to provide the power for the hydroelectric scheme built in the nineteen thirties. We cut across to Newton Stewart passing Clatteringshaws Loch, a man made loch constructed for the hydroelectric scheme, and through the Galloway Forest up to Loch Trool. The scenery is breath taking, and my parents were amazed at the vast expanse of forest, and the beauty of the region. This area is a well known beauty spot and attracts many visitors. Since that first visit with my parents we have visited that region many times, in all seasons, sunshine, rain and snow, and enjoyed walking in the hills. It was while climbing Merrick that I saw my first golden eagle.

On one of our days off the island, we explored new ground north of Dumfries, driving on gated tracks and discovering a large area with many sculptures scattered around. On enquiring we learned that these were the work of Henry Moore, a famous artist. I wonder if they are still there now, some forty three years later. It was good walking on the sands when the tide was out and enjoying picnics at Whiteport Bay, where we could swim. On one occasion we had walked off the island to Balcary and brought back a load of shopping, which we carried home over the mud flats. Eddie gave us half a dozen sand dabs for our tea, strung together on a piece of string, and my mother offered to carry the fish for us. About a third of the way across the dabs suddenly became very lively, and my mother dropped them in surprise, and declined to carry them any further. Nevertheless, she thoroughly enjoyed them for her tea.

In our garden we had a large patch of mint. One day I decided to make mint jelly. I had only made this previously with apples, but had found a good recipe using gelatine. I set my father the job of picking the mint leaves, stripping them from the stalks ready for me to mince them for the jelly. He read the recipe which clearly said use 2lbs of mint leaves. Some while later he appeared with two buckets full of mint leaves and even then there were not enough. I'm afraid there was a misprint and the recipe should have read '2 ounces' It was a pity to waste all that work and all those mint leaves, and we had plenty of gelatine and a sack of sugar, so I made vast quantities of mint jelly which lasted us for a long time, even though we used it liberally with most meals.

From the moment we bought our van we had to contend with a leak coming from somewhere in the roof, and although John worked on it several times, he could never find the origin of the leak. Unfortunately, when it rained the water always made a channel and dripped on whoever was sitting on the back seat, which on that first occasion was my father. On a wild, windy day, we walked off the island to Balcary and drove round to Colvend and along the coast road towards Dumfries. There are some lovely coves before reaching the popular beach at Sandyhills. The sea crashes against the rocks at Port O'Warren flinging the spray high. It is a spectacular sight. Down at the foot of the steep path leading to the small pebbly beach, there is a house. It was used as a holiday house at that time, and must have been a wonderful place from which to watch the fury of the storm.

Further along the coast at Southerness Point, there is a lighthouse situated on the long, wind-swept, sandy bay. Some years later Southerness was developed into a huge caravan park. On the day we visited Southerness with my parents there was a gale blowing. The sands were hard and there were tracks along the beach showing that cars drove along it. We took the van down and the wind was so strong that when the side doors were open the van was blown along the beach. Driving on the sands was a very unwise move, for we hit a soft patch of sand and the van became stuck. The tide was coming in, and I had visions of losing our newly acquired van to the Solway tide, followed by a long tiring walk of about twenty miles back to the island. We all pushed like mad, and eventually we gained the hard sand and made our way straight back to the metalled track. The tides on the Solway are very fast, and people have lost their lives by being caught by the tide, especially higher up the firth towards Annan. Mr. Houston told us a tale of one of the previous tenants who lost a cart load of furniture to the fast tide and the grand father clock was eventually washed up on the Cumberland coast at Whiteport.

Before John's parents arrived for a holiday, we had a week or two for more work on the outhouses and in the cottage. The calor gas cooker, made baking bread and cakes easy, a task which would have been very difficult on the old range. Our bedroom had a cast iron closed stove, and we moved this out of the bedroom into the sitting room to replace the decrepit range. Closed stoves are very efficient, giving out tremendous heat. Although drift wood washed up on the shore, this would not have been sufficient to keep the stove burning throughout the winter, and we ordered three tons of coal from the coal merchant in Dalbeattie. The week before John's parents arrived, the coal was delivered in hundred weight bags to the Fish house at Balcary, and we had the daunting task of shipping it over to Heston. There was a suitable place half way between the shore and the cottage where we could keep the coal and we started to bring the coal over in the dinghy. The boat could only accommodate a maximum of five bags at a time to be safe. It was hard work, especially for someone unused to lifting heavy weights. I dutifully held the floating dinghy, while John carried the sack of coal on his back and lowered it into the boat. By the third sack he was getting tired and as he reached the dinghy he lost his balance and grabbed the nearest thing, which was the dinghy. Of course, the dinghy moved towards him and John ended up sitting in the sea with the sack of coal still on his back! It was an hilarious sight, but John did not appreciate my laughter. The rest of the coal transportation was completed after John's parents arrived. Transporting the coal had turned our new immaculate boat into an unrecognisable dirty vessel and we needed to clean it, and ourselves thoroughly. The weather was good and after donning bathing costumes we sloshed water over the boat and ourselves until once again it was clean and fit for transporting our visitors. We knew that with its double hull our dinghy was very buoyant, and this proved to be very true as we struggled to tip the boat on its side to make its cleaning easier. This convinced us that the boat was unsinkable.

John's parents came by car and we had arranged to meet them at Balcary with the dinghy. That day the wind was strong and we could not steer the boat directly to the Balcary bay because of the strong currents. The boat eventually landed at Balcary after having been piloted north along the bay before finding shelter to come into the shore. John's mother was frightened of the sea, and although the wind had died down considerably by the time we had had coffee at the hotel, nothing would persuade her to climb aboard that tiny vessel. There was nothing for it but to wait until low tide and walk across the flats. We had learned that the safest way to cross on to Heston was by keeping well up the Balcary Bay, where the flats were firm. At a certain point we cut directly across towards the Almorness Point. Since those early journeys we have crossed over many times in the dark, and were able to cross the river in the shallowest, safest place by lining up with the black silhouette of one of the peaks on the Almorness peninsular. Once across the river we could aim for the rack of mussel covered rocks stretching out from the point of the island. Directly the distance from Heston to Balcary bay was less than a mile, but the route that was advisable for safety reasons was almost two miles. It was a long way to carry heavy cases, so John's parents just brought over the essentials for the night, and John motored over the next day for their luggage.

While mother enjoyed the rest and I did the daily chores, John and his father made trips over to the mainland to collect the remaining coal. The winds had dropped and the sea was a dead calm, which was just as well. To save another trip over, they loaded the final seven sacks onto the dinghy, and it was so low in the water that had there been any wave motion at all the dinghy would have been swamped. It was good to have our winter fuel safely stored. When winter arrived all the hard work of transporting the coal was made really worth while. Once the stove was lit it gave out tremendous heat. When there was a gale blowing it gave out so much heat that the outer wrought iron case glowed red hot. The fire never went out unless we were off the island for several days. At night it was banked up with slow burning dross and cooled down with a kettle of water if the wind was strong, and would remain alight for thirty six hours. There was one disadvantage, when it was first lit it filled the cottage with smoke, and it was necessary to open all the windows and doors and go for a walk for half an hour until the fog had cleared. The problem was probably due to the situation of the cottage. It was built on a ledge of rock jutting out from the hillside, and it faced north, looking across to the Scottish mainland. It had the advantage of being sheltered from the south-westerly gales, but produced a down draught in the chimney.

From our sitting room we had a wonderful view of the mainland hills, and the beauty of the sunsets reflected across the water. By July our tiny walled garden around the cottage was beautified by a patch of tall, orange, tiger lilies and two palm trees and a castor oil plant. There was also a New Zealand flax which we were told only flowers every five years, and luckily flowered for us in our first year. Our visitors often remarked on our tropical plants. We were told that the palm trees had come from the Isle of Man and were Norfolk Ireland palms from South Fiji. They grew a foot every year.

One day while we were on the mainland with John's parents, having coffee at the Balcary Hotel, we saw head lines emblazed across a paper being read by one of the guests. Our hearts sank; the building society to which we had entrusted our savings had gone bankrupt. We could do nothing about the situation, for all trading in that company had been suspended. This was a great blow, but we had had many set backs in life, and had learned to trust God for the future. In the event we did not lose our money, for the society was taken over by another building society, and our only loss was the interest for that one year.

John's father was a very good handyman, who was always willing to help; holidays for him were much more enjoyable if he had work to do. During their two weeks stay the work on the large byre was completed and made suitable for building organs. We already had an enquiry for a small organ from one of the local churches. Our plan was to build very small organs at a cost affordable for small churches. By using electric action, it was possible to use one rank of pipes ranging from very small pipes right up to the very large ones. This enabled several organ stops of different pitches to be taken from the one rank of pipes. With the old lever action, and pneumatic action, the pipes could only be used for one stop. The system we used did not produce such a rich tone, but had the advantage of being much cheaper to produce and enable small churches to enjoy the beauty of a pipe organ. In those days the smallest organ was priced at £250. I had a small hand printing press, and produced leaflets to advertise our organs and also offered maintenance and tuning work. The first two small organs were installed in local churches, and a few years back I visited these churches and they were still in use.

As well as parents, we had many day visitors who came over with the mussel men, and stayed for several hours. Some of these visitors were bird watchers, and enjoyed lying at the top of the cliffs observing the different types of gulls and sea birds, wheeling and diving into the sea. There were many different species of ducks, especially in the winter. The eerie call of the Great Northern Diver could be heard, and there were guillemots, golden eyed ducks and other sea birds that I could not identify. We also had visits from historians who were interested in the history of Heston and the surrounding region. It was interesting talking with our visitors and we learned a lot about the birds and history of the area. Most visitors were very considerate, knowing that it was a private island, they took themselves up over the hill to have their picnics. One or two were insensitive, peering into the cottage windows and even sitting on our doorstep for their picnic. They even asked us to boil water for them, so that they could make hot drinks. I don't think that they had any idea of the work involved in pumping up the drinking water, or carrying over the gas cylinders. As new comers to island life, we were very aware of the dangers of the sea, and always treated it with respect. On several occasions that first summer we were horrified by the actions of some of the visitors who came out to Heston in small boats. There were many hazards around Heston. Once the tide had covered the rack, a stranger would be unaware if there were a few inches of water over it, or several feet. Also jagged rocks which were submerged when the tide came in, were a great danger to boats whose skippers were unaware of the geography of the water around Heston. On one occasion we watched a father with two small children cut across the newly covered rack at great speed in his sporty speed boat. They then zoomed round the back of the island and came into the shore driving into the shell bank, leaving their boat while they clambered over the island. While they were gone I looked at the boat and noted that they had no oars, spare petrol, or anchor and rope. Neither the father or children were wearing life jackets. Fortunately, their stay on the island was brief and the tide had only risen a little. If they had been longer the boat would have floated away, for they had not bothered to secure it, or lift it above the tide.

One family who came to stay at the Balcary Hotel every year, had bought their young son a speed boat, and he could be seen with his friends racing over the rack and round the island at all states of the tide. We wondered how long the boat would last before he wrecked it. On one trip through rough sea they were getting drenched and proceeded to cover themselves right over their heads with a tarpaulin, and continued through the waves blindfolded. Apparently, the lad ripped the bottom out of the vessel on one of his outings, by coming into the bay at full speed and being unable to stop in time before hitting the rocks. Late in the summer we had a couple of youngsters arrive in a small row boat asking permission to camp on the island for a couple of nights. The weather was calm like a mill pond when they arrived, but the weather had deteriorated during their stay. The morning they were setting off for Kippford, there was a gale blowing, and we advised against their leaving the island, for the sea was too rough for a row boat. They would not listen, and insisted on setting out. They were certain that they could row to Almorness and then round into Rough Firth, where they would be able to hoist a coat on an oar and have an easy sail up to Kippford. They were rowing against the wind and the tide and were making no headway. I felt sure that they would return and stay another night, but they probably had too much pride to admit that they should not have risked setting out. They must have been drenched and very tired as they struggled against the elements, and it was a wonder that they were not swamped. At last they gave up, and turned back, but not to return to Heston, they made their way to the bay at Balcary. The next day we saw Eddie, and he asked if we knew anything about the small boat that had been beached and abandoned at Balcary. We told him the story and he was amazed that they had not been drowned.

Our first summer was coming to an end, and I was pleased with the work we had accomplished in the few months that we had been tenants. Our cottage was clean, newly decorated, even though rather garish, and some of the byres were repaired, and the garden producing food. Now the holiday season was over we had much work to do if we were going to earn a living.

Chapter 8 **Island Routine and Smuggling.**

"Whatever you do, work at it with all your heart, as working for the Lord."
(Colossians ch. 3 v 23.)

After a couple of months of really hard work to make our new home presentable
to our visitors, and comfortable for ourselves, we needed to plan for our future
living. It was good not being governed by time. Our lives had always depended on routine, set times for work, meals, recreation and sleep. Island life was
different, there was no 'nine till five' syndrome, but of course, there had to be a
certain amount of routine. It was necessary each night to check that the light
house was working, and giving out the right sequence of flashes. We could not
see the light from the cottage, but it came into view as we climbed up to the top
of the hill, and whatever the weather, this nightly journey was necessary. When
we were off the Island for a night, or at the weekend, we still needed to check
the light, and if there had been a gale and the light was out, then we made our
way back to Heston as quickly as possible.

There was not much shipping in the area; the Dutch boats came up to Palnackie
with a load of fertiliser fairly regularly, and there were fishing boats out on the
Solway Firth. The light was also used by aircraft in the region, so it was important that it was always flashing. On the occasions when we left the district to
visit our parents down south, the first thing we did on arrival was to call at the
local police station to report our temporary address, in case the light went out.
When giving the light house address, we were always careful to spell out the
name of the shire; KIRKCUDBRIGHSHIRE is pronounced kirkoobreeshire. I
remember one occasion giving our address, and the address of the lighthouse,
carefully spelling it out, much to the irritation of the policeman on duty, who
happened to come from Kirkcudbrightshire and knew the spelling far better than
I did. Each week the light house mechanism needed to be checked and the lamp
kept clean, and household and gardening tasks were ongoing. It was necessary
to leave the island at weekends for church, and also for buying our provisions.
Church, obviously, had a set time, and since leaving the island depended on the
weather and state of the tide, it was not easy to be certain of being there on time.
First of all this was overcome by leaving the island on foot or by boat, according to the weather, at any time, early or late dependent on the tide.

Before John officially became church organist for Colvend and Southwick, we
attended the Auchencairn kirk when this fitted the weather and the tides. The
Auchencairn church was a typical Scots kirk, with the pulpit occupying the cen-
tral position and the organ and choir stalls to the side. We wanted to worship at

61

Colvend, and John was keen to be the organist, a job he had held in churches from the age of fifteen; the £80 per year would also be useful. This meant that we needed to make sure that we could transport ourselves to the mainland in good time for the Sunday Services. We had become used to rising at all hours to rescue the fish from the hooks before the seagulls beat us to it, so we were happy to leave the island early or late. We managed by making our way over to the Balcary fish house, either by boat or walking the flats, according to the weather and tide, or sailing over to Rockcliffe. It was quicker to sail over to Rockcliffe when the weather and tides were suitable, and since the church was only a short walk away, we did not need the car. The minister lifted us in his car for the second service at Southwick. At this church I was surprised that there was only one person in the choir and he never opened his mouth. My curiosity got the better of me, and I asked someone why there was only one choir member and he did not sing. Laughter greeted my question, the side pews were not choir stalls, but the place where the local laird sat, and the man occupying it was the laird and also the local member of parliament. Apparently, he not only never opened his mouth in church, but was also renown for never opening his mouth in parliament. From Balcary we had a thirty mile round trip by road to reach Colvend and Southwick, using our own car. It was a long journey considering that we could clearly see the church over the water from Heston. The church was made even more visible to us just after we arrived, as the tower was repaired with copper sheeting, which gleamed in the sunlight, and clearly identified the building for miles around. It was not possible to reach Colvend clinging to the shore line, but necessitated driving into Dalbeattie to cross the River Urr by the bridge, and then coming down to the coast through the village of Barnbarroch. When the weather was bad in the winter, we often stayed over at the manse. This also meant that we could buy in our supplies while we were off the island for the weekend, and saved an extra journey.

On one occasion we were prevented from being at church while John was organist. There was a gale blowing and there was no way that we could risk the journey to the mainland in our twelve foot dinghy. At certain periods the tides, neap tides, did not go out as far as usual, and if there was a gale blowing, the rack did not clear and we remained an island for several days. We could not leave Heston either by boat or walking off. We had no means of letting the minister know that we would not be at church. Someone would be needed to play the organ at both churches, and also take Sunday School, for by this time I was the Sunday School teacher. Recently we had been fascinated by stories on the radio concerning the adventures of the Danish man, Tor Heyadol, who had built a boat made of reeds held together by rope. His theory was that it was in such vessels that men had sailed from the mainland to inhabit the Pacific islands. He had built his catamaran and had sailed it to prove his theory. Because of our interest in boats, it was fun to build a model of Heyadol's boat, the Kon Tiki, out of drift wood. A message was written and attached to the boat, saying that we were unable to be at church because of the gales, and we set it off in the direction of Rockcliffe. We watched our wee catamaran sail towards Rockcliffe for about a mile, then it was caught by the in-going tide. Through the telescope we watched it skirt along Rough Island and then head in the wrong direction, and we gave up watching it. It surprised us that our wee model did not sink or was not blown out to sea, for this is what we expected would happen, instead it arrived safely. The whole of Rockcliffe had received our news, and all were eager to talk about it. In some miraculous way the wee boat had managed to survive from being caught by the rocks off Rough Island, and eventually escaped the current and sailed into the rocks below the Mote of Mark, an old fort on the coast. Two lasses playing on the shore at Rough Bay, found our little boat stuck on the rocks and had waded out to retrieve it. They read the message, and in great excitement dashed three-quarters of a mile to the manse to tell the minister. Our model catamaran had sailed up Rough Firth and reached its destination, a crossing of about three miles, even though it had been tossed about and buffeted by the wild sea.

After the problem of being unable to leave the island because of the weather, we did start to think about how we would deal with an emergency on the island. Notifying our friends with a message attached to the improvised model catamaran, had been fun and had worked. We very well knew that that was a fluke, and was unlikely to work on another occasion. Both of us were very healthy, but we were aware that accidents or other crises could occur. Perhaps we could send a signal in an emergency, by lighting a bonfire, but even if it were seen from the mainland, they may not realise that it was a distress signal. Stories have been written about people living in desolate places becoming ill, and the hardship they endured when illness or accident struck them. Fortunately, we were never in that position, although there was one episode, that at the time was worrying. Later in life John developed both hay fever and migraine, and his first bout of migraine occurred on Heston, although we did not recognise it.

One day on returning from the mainland, John felt very ill, with a blinding headache and tremendous feeling of nausea, although he was unable to be sick. He went to bed hoping that it would pass, but it became worse. I had no idea what was wrong, but it did occur to me that perhaps he had eaten something that had poisoned him. I wondered whether to risk taking the boat to the mainland to try to get to a doctor, but the sea was very rough, and I was unused to handling the boat in rough weather. Another problem was, that at that time I had not learned to drive, and had no driving licence. Because John was feeling ill we had not lifted the dinghy up to the top of the beach, but had left it to be lifted later when John's sickness had passed. When evening came and the tide was rising fast, I realised that it would reach the dinghy, and if I did nothing about it, the rough sea would batter the bottom out of the boat. I went down to the shore and tried to drag the boat up the steep beach, but it defeated me. The only thing was to get John out of bed to help me, in spite of his weakness. He struggled into his clothes and staggered down to the sea. The stones and shells on the beach had been heaped up by the previous high tide almost vertically, and it took a lot of effort for both of us to lift the boat out of the sea's reach. The effort made John violently sick, but it made him feel immediately better, although still weak and washed out. The awful feeling of sickness had been relieved.

The stony, shell beach made it impossible to keep a bigger boat on the island, and the gales and rough seas would have made it difficult to anchor a boat off shore. After we left Heston and lived in Kippford, John built a flat bottomed catamaran, the size was immaterial, for we could easily drag it down to the sea on the thick gooey mud that was uncovered at low tide. The mud did have many disadvantages, however, as I experienced on several occasions. Certain parts were so soft that it was difficult to extract my boots from it, and I have fallen in the mud several times. At the top end of Kippford, where the river is flanked by the merse, there are a number of muddy gullies. One day we watched two children, thoroughly enjoying themselves. They had been paddling in the shallow water and on trying to climb out of the water had discovered the lovely mud. They then proceeded to enjoy themselves sliding down the mud banks into the water below. They were eventually hauled off by irate grandparents to be thoroughly sluiced down. A number of years later, our own two children found the delights of Kippford mud. Fortunately, the mud never stained our clothes, if we allowed it to dry, it could be brushed off.

In the months before we moved on to Heston we had spent the time planning what we should do. The island looked fertile, and we thought that we could buy a small tractor and plough up part of the land to grow vegetables. Tales had been told to us of the good crops that McWilliam had grown, and Tweedie his predecessor, 'the carrots were as long as your arm' we were told. Tweedie had also kept cows and used a horse to drag the plough and to take him to Castle Douglas on Saturday nights for his regular evening of drinking with his pals. The story goes that the horse knew the way back from the pub, crossing the mud flats, the lane and the rack without guidance. Every Saturday night after Tweedie was drunk, his drinking partners would load Tweedie into the cart and give the horse a whack. The horse would then set off and deliver his owner safely to the cottage on Heston, by which time the fresh air and jolting would wake Tweedie sufficiently to clamber out of the cart and greet his wife.

As already mentioned we had borrowed books from our local library on small hold farming, and machinery, and sent off for catalogues. This idea was short lived, for we had notification from the owners that we could only plough up a small area of land. The reason given being that they wanted to keep an ecological balance on the island, and growing crops might upset this. Since the island had been neglected, both in Houston's time and the last part of McWilliam's tenancy, bracken had become out of control, and covered half of the island. Ploughing up part of the island would probably have helped the ecological balance, but the owners were adamant and we needed to rethink our plans. We gave up the idea of farming the island, for it would not be worth buying in expensive equipment just for half an acre of land. We had also been advised that it would be too risky to keep cows with unfenced cliffs. There would also be the problem of transporting the milk daily to the mainland, whatever the weather. The only option left to us was to be content with growing as much food as possible in the walled gardens, and find another way of making a living.

After our disappointment regarding farming the island, we concentrated our thoughts on turning John's love for organs from being a hobby to becoming a profitable business. The business was planned so that we could build small organs for village churches, and also set up an organ tuning round. Our new business was to be called Solway Organs. Over the summer the byres at the far end of the cottage were made weatherproof, and suitable for building organs. There was plenty of space. We already owned many tools, in those days, unfortunately, they had to be hand tools, since we had no electricity. When the organ business began to take off, we bought a generator for use in the workshop, for we needed to test the electrical action. The large barn had an earthen floor with remains of an ancient threshing mill which had rotted away. The building next to this was smaller and had housed the mill, it had a concrete floor. This was the most suitable for a workshop, and work was started on it early so that it would be in good order ready for the winter. John had worked in research since leaving school, and this ability enabled him to plan and work out a system of making pipe organs that even small churches could afford. He had explored the idea of building extension pipe organs, and experimented on the best type of action for enabling air from the wind chest to be channelled and operated, so that each pipe could be used to its full potential.

One of our first paid jobs, was to repair the pipe organ at Colvend. The tools we needed were carried over the mud flats to the fish house, since we could not rely on the weather for sailing across to Balcary. The tides that week meant that it was late at night when we managed to walk off the island, and by the time we had driven round to Colvend it was nearly midnight. We worked through the night to complete the repair. Our work routine was geared to the state of the tide, paying no regard to clock time. Our first paid work was very satisfying and we drove back to Balcary, garaged the van in the fish house, and as soon as possible started our walk across the sands. Even in the middle of the night it was never completely dark, we were always able to make out the dark shapes of the hills. The sands were always wet and in any case we had the river to cross, so until the weather became too cold, we walked bare foot across the flats. That morning it was still dark and the water on the flats and in the river was icy cold. We were walking towards the sunrise and were guided by the outline of the Almorness peninsular, about a mile and a half away. It was important to aim for the correct hump on the peninsular, the Moyl of Almorness, and not to become confused with Barcloy hill, three miles away on the other side of Rough Firth. This mistake would lead us too high up the bay and too near the quick sands for our liking.

It was wise always to carry a compass and a whistle when we walked the flats, in case a sea mist came rolling in, or we got into difficulties, but we never needed to use them. A powerful torch was also carried, but it was not much use on the flats because of the surface layer of the water which reflected the light upwards. In any case, using a torch blinded our night vision. As the Almorness peninsular loomed nearer, we knew that we were approaching the lane, and walked cautiously, feeling for the edge, and then using our sticks to probe the bottom and avoid the pot holes. It was quite nerve racking crossing the river at night, as we could not see the far side, and we never knew how wide it was, as it varied in width and depth according to the water draining from the merse. The current tugged at our ankles, especially as we neared the deepest part, and we could only see the black swirling water pouring passed us as we carefully made our way to the far bank.

Once we were over and had scrambled up the bank, we were on firm sand and walked parallel to the black shadow of land on our left and towards the rack. As we rounded the point, Heston was a black silhouette against the lightening sky. The rack did not stretch all the way to the point, the last part faded into sands. If we walked too far to the left we could see the Heston light, and would be able to rectify our course. I did use the torch once we were on the rack, for it helped to pick out the larger boulders and avoid stumbling over them. On this occasion by the time we reached the rack we were able to watch the dawn breaking, clear and cold. There were many seagulls feeding on the rack, gobbling up the unsuspecting sea life that the receding tide had left exposed. Other gulls were circling overhead, their wild, plaintive cries breaking the quietude of that magical morning hour.

Winter treks over the flats were not easy; as well as battling against the wind and rain, we were dressed in trawler coats and thigh boots to protect us from the elements, and they were heavy, and often our heavy back packs added to the struggle. There was one notable crossing that gave us great concern. We had been off the island for a couple of days and needed to return to make sure that the sheep were all safe. There was a souwesterly gale blowing and the tides were dropping to the neap period, when sometimes the rack would not uncover. With this gale we knew that we must walk onto the island that evening, for it was almost sure that by the next tide we would be unable to get over. The burn feeding the lane was in spate with the winter rains, which made the current very strong, so it was advisable to cross the lane at the latest possible time so that the volume of water would be less. It was also necessary to catch the tide at its lowest point, especially as on that day there was a possibility that the sea would not leave the rack completely. As we neared the water we could see that the tide had not left the lane, and the water spread out from it over a wide area. We walked higher up the bay but the water still spread out widely. As we were anxious to reach Heston, we decided that we must make an effort to cross. As we crossed the water rose higher up our thigh boots. If the water had threatened to go over the top of our boots we would have turned back, and hoped that the sheep were safe, for it would have been too dangerous to cross. The way across was aided by our sticks, as we carefully felt ahead for ruts and holes. The water was getting very near the top of my boots before we started to rise. We crossed the deepest part of the lane and the water was less deep.

This diversion had wasted time and the tide was coming in and had reached the Almorness rocks, but we could see the rack still clear of the water, about a quarter of a mile away. We waded over the sands through about an eighteen inch depth of sea, and as we came out of the shelter of the Almorness point we met the breaking seas rolling up the bay between Heston and Balcary. The waves broke against us as we braced ourselves, and I was glad to have a stick for support. As we walked towards the rack, to our dismay, we seemed to be facing a losing battle, for the sea was gradually covering the rack. The uncovered area was receding, and the water was getting deeper. If we could not battle against the sea it would be wise for us to return to the Almorness Point and spend the night there. It would have been impossible to cross back over the lane as the tide was rising fast. Having come this far, we were determined to try to make it across. Once onto the rack the water became shallower, and we were able to walk along more quickly and keep pace with the rising water. It was necessary to make sure that we kept in the centre of the rack, for if we had strayed off the rack the water each side would have been too deep for us. Once on the rack we knew that the worst was over, and thanked God for his protection in making Heston in safely. Apparently, a previous tenant had crossed over much later than this to reach home, and had actually been washed off his feet by the sea when crossing the rack, but had made it safely.

That day we had taken a risk, but a risk based on our knowledge of the tides, the lane and the rack, learned from many crossings, but others without this knowledge have been in trouble. Eddie told us of a visitor, who had so enjoyed the wonder and beauty of Heston, that she forgot all about the passing time. She at last realised that she had stayed longer than the time advised by those at the hotel where she was staying. She was not aware of the danger of the tides, and happily started to gather up her belongings ready to return to the mainland. When she realised the tide was coming in fast, she panicked, not wanting to spend the night on the island alone, for there was no one at that time in residence. In spite of the tide coming in swiftly, she left the island and on reaching the lane crossed over with the water up to her chest. It was summer, the weather was calm and the lane had not been gauged out into pot holes, had this not been so, she could have drowned.

Young people enjoy the adventure and challenge of life, and we certainly revelled in all our experiences of Heston, and found great satisfaction in it. Life on the island was not all struggling with the elements, or hard work. After spending a weekend of comfort with our friends at Colvend, they often commiserated with us, having to return to the privation of island life. It was not like that, whatever the weather we enjoyed it. It was the breath of life to us. I have stood on the flats with a Force 10 gale lashing my body, my face stinging with hail stones, leaning on my stick away from the wind, watching the multitude of white hail stones running, skipping and bouncing across the flats, feeling part of the storm. This invigorating experience makes up for any discomfort. We also enjoyed the calm, peaceful times, like crossing over the flats at sunrise. We loved the peace and sanctuary of our island home and there was a great spiritual dimension to our lives bringing us closer to God. On Heston we were free, and as I look back over the years, I appreciate more and more that oasis in my life, and am grateful for the privilege of having experienced it.

There was still plenty of work to do, especially that we now needed to concentrate on making a living and earn our daily bread. The placing of the first order for a small pipe organ gave us the motivation we needed, and work began in earnest. All the parts necessary for building the organ were ordered and eventually dispatched and transported over to Heston. There was much cabinet making involved in organ building to make the finished product look good. We were able to obtain supplies of oak from a local builder. Much of the interior work used very strong sheets of material made from sawdust and resins. In our day it was called Weyroc, but this was probably a brand name. Fortunately, there was a factory making this type of wood in Annan, a town not far from Dumfries. It was used in building the chests where the pipes would stand and this was connected to the console by complicated electric magnet action. The various parts of the organ were built and the organ erected in the workshop. By using electricity from the petrol driven generator the various bits of the action were tested. Organ pipes can be made of metal or wood. The metal pipes were purchased, but we built the wooden pipes ourselves.

The problem now was how to transport the larger parts of the organ from Heston. The van was garaged at the fish house, but first the components must be ferried over from the island. If at all possible, we were determined to use our dinghy to transport the organ. The pipes, blower and smaller parts would be easy, and we hoped that even the larger parts could be successfully carried on a really calm day. The case of the organ was a box, five feet wide, four feet high and three feet deep. The organ case was carried down to the beach and laid flat across the gunwales of the dinghy, but it was still too high for John to see over as he sat at the tiller. It was a calm day and we decided to risk taking it across. I sat in the bow and called directions. At that time one of the comedy programmes on the radio featured the navy, and we had great fun in imitating the characters. "Left hand down a bit. No up a bit"; and "Stop engines" as we crunched onto the gently sloping beach of Balcary. This was the difficult part of transporting the case and we were very pleased at the easy trip, and thought the rest would be easy. The van was backed down onto the firm beach without any trouble; the beach was made up of well bedded stones. The case was slid off the boat into the van, and after lifting the dinghy to safety we were ready to go. That is when the fun began. As soon as we attempted to drive up the sloping part of the beach the surface disintegrated into loose pebbles. The only way to conquer the slope was by getting up a bit of speed along the level and then swinging up the slope as far as we could get, and turning before the grip was lost. This was repeated until at last we reached the top of the beach. Our first attempt at ferrying organ parts from the island, made us realise that we needed to find an alternative method of transportation, especially if our business grew. The large organ chest was much heavier than the case, and it was fitted out with expensive electrical equipment, and we could not afford to risk trying to transport it from the island ourselves. We decided to ask the help of the mussel men, for their boat was much bigger than ours and capable of carrying large loads. When we came back onto the island after a couple of days away, we would ask the men if they would take the chest up to Kippford for us on one of their trips, and we would come round in the van to meet them there. We were willing to pay them for the work. We had planned to stay off the island for a few days, and had warned the mussel men that we would not be home. In the event we returned to the island a day earlier than we had intended. The fishermen usually knew our movements, for on the days we were off they did not get their pot of tea. They looked a bit taken aback when we walked up the rack and greeted them, and one of them complained "Ah thocht ye was stayin' aff fo twae days." Instead of complaining, surely they should have been pleased at our arrival, for they would get their pot of tea. Then John asked them if they would be willing to transport the organ chest for us as it was too heavy for our dinghy. At our request we were amazed how they cheered up and were eager to help us. "It'll be a pleasure. Dinna gie it anither thocht. Ah'll tak' it up the village tae ma ane garage. Na, na, nae a penny", he protested as John tried to discuss terms. "It's ma pleasure." Glances passed between us as this was quite a surprise, and we wondered about their sudden generosity. As we thanked them and turned to make our way up to the cottage, one of the men called after us. We knew that there must be a catch, and there was. "Ah hope ye dinna min'? Ah've put a wee bit parcel in yere pigsty. It was nae convenient tae tak' it this trip." They promised to come out for the parcel when it was convenient. Having reassured him that we did not mind, since the pigsty was not used, we again made our way up to the cottage, wondering why it 'was not convenient' to take the parcel back with them.

The two men acted as pilots for the little coasters of three to five tons, which brought cargoes of raw fertiliser up to Palnackie, where it was unloaded. It was then transported to the mill at Dalbeattie to be processed. The coaster then took a load of timber back from Palnackie, or sometimes crossed the Firth to Workington or Whitehaven to collect a load of coal. The River Urr has very sharp bends and we were told that in the early days a new ship, on its maiden voyage, was blown onto the banks near Shennan Creek. At low tide she was perched on bow and stern on the mud banks. The skipper-owner was lucky that the vessel did not break her back, and never risked taking the boat up the Urr by himself again. The coaster would arrive in good time to catch high tide and anchor in Heston's east channel and wait for the pilot to come out. The two men would go out to meet the ship in their boat and one of them climbed aboard and piloted the vessel, while the other brought the motor boat back to Kippford. Our telescope was used a lot, we liked watching the birds, the yachts, the Cumberland coast on a clear day, and we had also seen the men meet the Dutch ship. We had noticed that the fishermen's boat always tied along side the ship on the side facing away from the mainland, and packages were lowered into the boat. No one from the shore could observe this, but we could from the island.

After the tide rose sufficiently and the men had finished picking mussels and made their way home, curiosity got the better of us and we went to the pigsty to see what we were harbouring. Having been off the island for a couple of days, we were not aware whether the coaster had sailed up to Palnackie or not. We suspected that it had been up the estuary, and the parcels might have come from the coaster and this made us rather anxious. Our only knowledge of smuggling was through the books we read, and we enjoyed reading the tales of The Reverend Doctor Sin. We sympathised with the hero, as we were meant to do, but we were aware that these adventures were just light hearted stories. Of course, we knew that in the past every little port had its smugglers, and in fact the Balcary Hotel had a colourful history of smuggling in the old days. I remember being shown a cottage in the hills above Auchencairn that could be seen from well out at sea. This was used to give signals to the men bringing the contraband ashore. Still, that was in the past, and being town dwellers we were unaware that smuggling still took place, we thought it was all in the past. Today, I am very aware of the problems of smuggling, especially drugs; but nearly fifty years ago I knew little about this, or other types of illegal activities that still occurred in the big city ports.

Our fears were realised when we looked into the parcels and found cigarettes, brandy and nylons. I then remembered the conversation we had had on one of our journeys over to Heston, when the men transported our furniture for us. The idea of setting up a still in one of the caves had not just been a passing obser-vation, but had been thrown out to see if we would react positively. Since mov-ing onto Heston, we had investigated the caves. Only one of the two caves half way up the cliff face in Copper Cove is accessible, the roof of the other one hav-ing caved in. There had been two other borings down on the shore, but these were covered with a tangle of briars. The cave, which was the old water supply, was deep and perhaps might have been suitable for an illicit trade. We had also investigated the cave on the south side of Heston, which Crockett greatly embellished in his story, The Raiders. When we had explored the cave we were quite impressed with its size but it was dark and gloomy, its floor littered with a pile of debris left behind by the winter gales. I'm not very keen on entering dark caves, which usually have water running down their slimy walls. This cave was no exception, and I remember when we visited it I was petrified. We had dis-turbed a colony of rock doves and these dark forms rushed past our heads, mak-ing for the cave opening like 'bats out of hell.' This cave was plenty large enough, but only easily accessible from the sea. The cave in mind was probably the one in Copper Cove, for this was hidden and yet fairly accessible, and perhaps suitable for setting up a still. As we looked at the contraband goods we were shocked. As tenants of the island we were responsible, and if any one discovered the goods we would be in a lot of trouble. Our first reaction was to hide the boxes, and this we did by piling empty crates and containers against them. We were puzzled why the men had left the parcels on the island. It was clear now, that the packages we had seen lowered from the ship while the motor boat was tied along side, were contraband goods. This had happened on a number of occasions, and presumably on the other occasions the goods had been taken straight up to Kippford.

The enigma was solved a few months later, when we had a visit from a reporter based in Glasgow. He asked us about our island life, but it was clear he had not come all this way to cover a story which was now old news. Eventually he came to the point, and asked us if we had heard the rumour that the Customs and Excise men had been taking an interest in Kippford. He wanted to know if it was true that the Yacht Club was suspected of being involved in smuggling. We answered honestly that we were not aware of the Custom's interest, or knew of any Yacht Club involvement. He then told us that a few months back the officials had been tipped off that a consignment was being shipped in, and men had been sent down to Kippford. This explained everything. I suppose normally they would have left the boxes in their boat on the mooring, and probably carried them ashore after dark. Impatiently, we waited for the tide to come up, and hoped that the men would come out as soon as there was enough water, and take their ill-gotten goods away. We found it difficult to settle, watching the sea for signs of the fishermen's boat. It began to get dark and the tide was ebbing and there was no sign of them. Then, with alarm, we saw a white cutter swinging out of Rough Firth round Horse Isles and Whiteport bay heading for Heston. We convinced ourselves that it must be the custom's men and tried to decide how we should handle the crisis. The best thing was just to tell them the truth, and hope that they would believe us.

As the cutter dropped anchor off shore, we made our way down to the beach and watched as a dinghy came towards us. A man approached us while another dragged the dinghy up the pebble shore. Then much to our relief we saw that the man dragging up the boat was one of the mussel men. Surely he would back up our story. It turned out that he was coming to collect the parcels with a friend to whom the yacht belonged. Later, we heard that the man owned one of the hotels in Dumfries, so we assume he was the one who bought the contraband. In our anxiety to remove the goods from the island as quickly as possible, we helped carry them down from the pigsty. We were offered a bottle of brandy, but refused, truthfully saying that neither of us drank alcohol. This episode was never repeated, and we were never again sounded out about keeping a still in the cave. We slept easily that night, thankful that our little adventure was over, without any repercussions.

Chapter 9 **Wintering Sheep.**

"All we like sheep have gone astray" (Isaiah chapter 53 verse 6.)

Our first summer and autumn passed, and with them the visitors who came to Heston. It was good to be alone, enjoying being free from visitors. We valued having our own family and taking time off to show them round the beautiful country side of Galloway, but it was not so much fun when the day trippers came. Many were fine, but quite a number were thoughtless and invaded our privacy, and worse, some endangered their own lives by their lack of respect for the sea. Now the autumn was here we were looking forward to the arrival of the sheep which wintered on the island each year. Heston island is a solid chunk of rugged rock sitting off the Scottish side of the Solway coast. Except for the northern point, the cliffs rear up all round the island, some a hundred feet high. The hill side slopes up from the cliffs quite steeply. You might expect it to be barren, but except for the steepest rocks, it is covered with rich, deep soil. In the winter, when the mainland pastures have been grazed bare, Heston is covered with succulent grass. The bracken is spreading in parts of the island and we tried to keep this in control by scything it down. We had a visit from the farmer at Nether Linkins which lies behind Bengairn, and we agreed to continue the tradition of wintering forty to fifty of his sheep. At the beginning of October a suitable date was fixed when the sheep could be driven over to Heston at low tide. The sheep were brought down from the farm several miles along an old hill track and then onto the sands near the Auchencairn end of the bay. I watched eagerly through my telescope awaiting their arrival, and at last saw the flock come down herded together on the sands by three sheep dogs. The dogs were very much needed, for there was a great stretch of sands on which they could easily have scattered. The sheep were kept closely together and as I watched they seem to flow across the flats, the moving shadow continually changing shape. When they reached the river they separated running along the bank, some trying to turn back. The dogs, farmer and shepherd kept the sheep together and tried to herd them across the river, but no amount of shouting, barking and snapping of the dogs, would induce them to enter that quick flowing water. We think of sheep as silly animals, but during our tenancy we came to realise that they were not as silly as we thought, they have a great instinct of self preservation. As I watched I saw the men each grab one of the sheep and lift them up, kicking and struggling, and carry them bodily over the river, while the dogs kept the rest from straying. I wondered if they were going to carry them all over, and that would have proved to be a tiring, lengthy task. However, a couple were sufficient. The rest of the flock saw the two sheep safely over on the other side, and heard their bleating and immediately waded into the water and crossed without hesitation. Once across the water the sheep again merged into a moving liquid pool which flowed across the sands onto the rack and made their way up to the island.

Mr. Houston had a sheep dog to help round up the sheep each day. He warned us never to let the sheep stray down onto the shore in case they wandered over the rack and off the island at low tide, or got drowned. As we had no dog and did not want to spend our whole time penning the sheep up on the hill, we were hoping that the sheep would stay on the hill of their own accord. Mr Houston rarely left the island, and other than the responsibility of the lighthouse, had nothing else to do all day. Having spent a week with him in April, we knew that he kept odd hours, and often slept for several hours in the day, the dog usually with him. There must have been opportunities for the sheep to come down to the shore when the old man was unaware of it, so we just hoped that it was not necessary for us to act as jailors to a flock of sheep. There was no need for us to worry, for in the three years we wintered sheep we only lost one of them, and that was beyond our control, and nothing to do with the sheep coming down to the water's edge. The sheep were Black-faced hogs, that is they were adolescent sheep with black faces, long, curling horns and shaggy, woolly coats reaching the ground. This breed of sheep is very common in Scotland, being hardy, and not needing a lot of attention. The disadvantage is that their coats easily get tangled in brambles, briars and blackthorn. There were no trees on Heston, but plenty of brambles and briars growing on the cliff and on the ledges and crevices. Sometimes they formed an impenetrable jungle, and the sheep seemed to delight in getting themselves well and truly enmeshed in the bramble thickets. Their heavy coats also became very heavy when there had been much rain, and like most of the west of Britain, we had plenty of rain. If the sheep rolled on their backs to scratch in wet weather, they found it very difficult to get up again because of the weight. This made it imperative that they were counted at least every three days, the time limit for recovering a healthy animal. Handling sheep was difficult. On the few occasions when a sheep needed to be lifted on its feet, it seemed as if the animal were paralysed, lying deadly still, but as soon as it was lifted up it struggled madly until its legs buckled and it was on the ground again. It took about ten minutes struggling with the animal, until the strength returned in its legs and it was able to stumble away and start to feed. Few needed to be rescued when on their backs, but it was a common occurrence to have to cut sheep free from the brambles.

The sheep usually grazed together, so counting them was not too difficult, but there always seemed to be one of the flock that was awkward, and made it necessary to scour the whole island to see where it was trapped. There seemed to be loyalty amongst the sheep, and we have been guided to a lost animal by the running and bleating of one near by. If we had been off the island for the week-end, then it was a priority to count the sheep before doing anything else. We were usually already tired by the time we reached the island, sometimes having walked two miles battling against a strong wind, and carrying a heavy back pack. We were equipped with good waterproofs and thigh boots, for in the winter the river could be quite deep, and there is nothing worse than having a wellington boot filled with water. The waterproof trawler coats were cumbersome, and underneath were layers of woollen jumpers and a jacket, to keep out the cold winds, but these and a couple of pairs of woollen socks kept us snug what ever the weather. There were times when we could actually lean on the wind with our full weight and remain upright. One of the worst conditions for crossing the flats was a combination of strong winds and rain or hail, the tremendous squalls would drive over the sands, hurling stinging hail stones which bounced around us, and we became part of the storm. Only our faces were exposed to the elements and the force of the wind caused even the rain to sting our faces as the drops felt like pellets fired from a gun. My mother knitted us balaclavas which we wore in very bad conditions, but they always seemed claustrophobic and itchy. In spite of the tiring walk across the flats it was also very exhilarating. It was a great thrill knowing that you were alone in the wildness, pitting your strength against the wild elements. Living on Heston was a great physical challenge to be enjoyed, as well as absorbing the spiritual awareness of the beauty of God's creation and the tremendous feeling of space.

One January morning there was a freezing drizzle being driven over a grey sea by a strong east wind, which penetrated our very bones. I had stayed in while John went to count the sheep. He was away for a long time, and eventually came back with the news that one sheep was missing, and he had looked hard and long, but could not find it. I clambered into my waterproofs and set out with him to search again. We eventually discovered the missing animal, it was in a bramble thicket about twenty feet down the cliff beyond the lighthouse. I brought up the rope and anchor from the boat and we securely embedded the anchor into the strong turf above the cliff. While John climbed down the rope, I sat on the anchor to make sure that it was firmly embedded. I saw John try to grab the sheep by its horns, but in fright it jumped out of the way and fell another ten feet. The rope was not long enough to reach the lower ledge, and John climbed back up the rope. Perhaps we could reach the sheep by scrambling down the slippery rocks where the cliffs were less steep, and clambering round the base of the cliff to effect a rescue by climbing up to the ledge from the bottom. This was duly tried but was too difficult. The driven rain was intensified by the salt spray being flung against the rocks, and with no hand holds to enable a climb up the cliff, we had to abandon this attempt at rescue. If John had slipped the possibility of his falling onto the jagged rocks, or into the sea, was not worth taking a chance. There were some salmon net poles by the cottage, twelve feet long, and as we returned to the cliff top, we carried a pole with us. Once again I sat on the anchor, by this time very wet, while John climbed down the rope once more bearing the long pole. There was nothing for it, but to aim the pole at the sheep to push it off the ledge, hoping that the fall to the rocks below would not kill it. She dropped a good thirty feet and landed on her feet, and wandered off happily, making her way over the rocks to the north bay and climbed up the path to join the rest of the herd.

On another occasion it was becoming dusk as we returned onto the island, and the sheep still needed to be checked. It was very tempting to leave the count until the following day, but in spite of our tiredness we knew the job must be done. After counting the main flock twice there were still seven missing. As we searched the cliffs, calling the sheep, there were none to be seen and no responding bleats. It was getting late and we were beginning to feel desperate, wherever could they be, we had searched the whole island, peering over the cliffs to check the ledges and the coves. John then hand a very strange experience, which he had never had before or since. He had asked God's help and clearly heard a voice in his mind saying, "Climb down into Copper Cove." His reaction was to reject the advice, for we had already looked down into the cove and there were no sheep visible. The words came to him again "Go down." He struggled down the hundred feet of steep path, and there, invisible from the top of the cliffs, were two sheep caught in briars just inside the entrance of one of the bore holes. There were still five sheep missing, and again he prayed "Where now?" The answer came, "Straight up the cliffs and over the hill." The cliff rose steeply, but he struggled up to the top and over the hill to the corner of the path out onto the pinnacle of rock. As he looked down he could see five sheep huddled in the brambles under an overhang of rock that he had never noticed before. They were soon rescued, and returned to the flock. I have never had an experience like that, my guidance coming in more normal and explainable ways, but certainly the words John heard in his mind answered our desperate need, for it would have been a disaster to lose seven of the flock.

Only one sheep was lost in the three years we wintered them, and its loss was a mystery which we never solved. On this occasion we searched every nook and cranny of the island, and even motored round the island, scanning the cliff face for signs of a trapped animal. We continued the search for several days and finally gave up believing that the sheep must have fallen off the cliffs and drowned. Much to our astonishment, about a fortnight after its disappearance we discovered it lying on the open flat area of the island near the lighthouse. It was dead, yet there was no signs of it having struggled with brambles. The fleece was in perfect condition. Another day when one of the flock was missing and could not be found, we abandoned the search as it was getting dark, but continued to look the next morning. There was still no trace of it. As we were walking back along the cliffs, having given up all hope, we heard a weak bleat. The sheep could only be seen by lying on the top of the cliff and leaning over. It had been caught in the brambles and tried to free itself without success. It was tethered to the bramble and in its hunger had circled round on the ledge eating whatever food was in reach. As it circled the fleece had become wound round the bramble until it made a thick rope of wool. The more it circled the thicker the fleece rope and this had wound its back legs off the ground. It was a pitiful sight, bleating with its back legs waving futilely in the air. The fleece was badly damaged as we cut it away to free the sheep. A friend on Unst, the northern most Shetland island, was asked how he rescued his sheep from the cliffs. He said they were left to their own devices, and they usually managed to scramble down the cliffs and find their own way back to the flock. They were able to do this, for no brambles or briars grew on the island to ensnare the poor animals. We often wished that Heston was free from brambles.

As well as causing a lot of hard work, the sheep also gave us a great deal of pleasure. Many mornings as we sat by the window eating our breakfast, the sheep kept us amused. We heard the clunk of their hooves as they passed by the cottage each morning, on their way to the shore. They paddled in the sea pools nibbling the sea weed. In one of the gales a large tree branch was washed near the shore, and we dragged it up onto the beach to dry out to be used as fire wood. It lay there with part of the branch sticking up into the air. The sheep discovered it, it was just the right height for them to walk underneath and use as a rubbing stump. They queued up, taking it in turns to slide backwards and forwards under the crook of the branch in a state of euphoria. When the sheep next in line thought it was her turn she gave a gentle nudge, and moved into place and proceeded to scratch her back on the branch with great delight. This behaviour became a ritual and was part of the morning visit, before they returned to the hill to resume their grazing.

When the sheep were brought onto the island some of them were limping with foot rot. One year one of the hogs was carried on because of a badly damaged foot. Mr. Houston's sheep were still affected with foot rot when they went off the island in the spring. In the three years we wintered sheep, not one left the island with foot rot, not even the ones that had come on limping. Sea water has a great healing power, and I feel sure that by allowing the sheep to come down each day and paddle and eat the sea weed, they were kept healthy. This also proved true for me. I developed a red patch on my skin, and the doctor prescribed a sulphur ointment to cure it. After many weeks there was no improvement. When the water had lost its winter chill, I went swimming each day in Copper Cove, and within a few weeks the skin had healed. I read somewhere, that the sheep on Ronaldsay, one of the Orkney islands, were fenced off the island, and their only food came from grazing the seaweed on the shore. This continued until oil pollution made it unsafe for them.

The sheep we wintered were hogs, so there were no lambs on Heston. On one of our days off, I encountered a very special lamb. We had driven up into the Glenken hills north of the village of New Galloway, and as we walked one of the lambs from the flock of sheep came to investigate me. I bent down to stroke it. I think this must have been the first very young lamb that I had ever touched, for I was very surprised by the stiffness of its wool. I always thought of lambs with soft, cuddly coats. We moved on, but the lamb decided to come with us. After a while I was worried that it would get lost, as its mother did not call it back. Shooing had no effect, so we decided to run as fast as we could to lose the lamb. The lamb could run as fast as we could, so that was a waste of energy. My next ploy was to run and then lie down flat, keeping perfectly still, so that the lamb would lose interest. When the lamb caught up with me, it climbed on my back, curled up and went to sleep. Eventually the lamb became tired of its new mum, and skipped off back to find its real mother.

When we spent time in the Glenkens we tracked down the wild goats. These days they are penned in so that they cannot wander too far, but in the nineteen fifties they roamed over a wide area. There were usually young kids with them. Towards the end of our tenancy of Heston, when the organ building business was prospering, we needed a base on the mainland, and bought a wee cottage in Dalbeattie. We discovered how playful kids are, watching the antics of our neighbour's goats and their two small white kids. They used to climb onto the galvanised roof of a barn and skip up and down, revelling in the noise their little hooves made. One day John had laid out all his equipment and organ parts on the lawn, ready to load into the van. In the few minutes he disappeared into the cottage, one of the kids escaped and ended up amongst John's equipment, causing havoc. One of the fully grown billy goats managed to find its way to Dalbeattie Primary School on one occasion, joining the children in the play ground. The teacher was a friend of mine, and told me that she thought the children were winding her up, but no the goat had happily made itself at home with the children.

Chapter 10   **Winter.**

"O ye frost and snow, bless ye the Lord."   *(Song of the three holy children :-*
Apochrypha.)

When the onset of our first winter came we were unprepared. We had not been
off the island for several days, and suddenly the weather changed and it became
very cold and an icy grip was laid on our world. The engine of the Bond-Mini
had been air cooled; but now it was necessary to drain the radiator of the van, if
we were to avoid damage from frozen water. The radiator had not been drained,
and we decided to drag the boat down, and motor over to the fish house. It was
a pleasure being on the sea in the dark, if the weather were good. We wrapped
up for the winter night, and there was a layer of ice covering the boat as we
dragged it down the moonlit beach. The shells heaped up by the gales, crackled
under our feet and the dinghy's keel. The sea was mirror calm, and the boat
slipped into the water and floated gently. The mainland encircled the bay and
we could see the lights shining from the farmhouse windows giving us guidance
to the fish house cove.

The sea had many moods, and we grew to love it, whether it was lashing the
cliffs for days on end, or sleeping in the icy calm of a winter's night. At first it
was good to drift gently on the unruffled water; even the gulls whose raucous
cries usually shattered the peace were quiet, some on the shore sleeping peacefully with heads tucked into fluffed feathers. There was work to be done, so the
engine was started and we drove over to the bay and drained the water from the
radiator of the van, and then prepared to return home. The noise from the outboard shattered the peace of the night, and we switched off the motor and floated noiselessly on the surface of the water. The sea was so calm that every star
was reflected in the water, and we moved between the brilliant moon, high
above, and its reflection in the sea. The light in the sky was beautiful, delicate
beams of translucent green floated upwards and died away. Gradually the green
light in the sky towards the north became an ethereal curtain of auroral light,
which sank below the hills. Imperceptibly the sky reddened with a clear light
through which the stars still shone undimmed. The red light increased in inten-
sity, filling the whole sky, with the sea reflecting an eerie crimson glow. The
whole world seemed to be on fire, and in awe and wonder we drifted watching
this wonderful display of the Northern Lights. It was well passed midnight
when we motored gently back to our island home, thankful for the privilege
granted to us to behold this wonder of nature. Living on Heston had made us
acutely aware of the vastness of the sky, but tonight both sky and sea had fused
into one. As we moved through the water the bow wave parted the crimson sea,

leaving behind us a silvery, red wake. The bow slithered onto the shore, and we stood there watching the moon as it slipped behind the hills, and waited as the red light faded and once again the land returned to its darkness, the hills darkly silhouetted against the sky.

This was the beginning of a severe winter. Our island was featured on the front page of the local newspaper. For the first time in living memory, Heston was covered with a blanket of snow, transforming the familiar green island that guarded the entrance to Rough Firth. That winter was hard and cold and ice flows covered with snow from the night's blizzard, lifted off the merse at the head of the bay and floated out to sea. As we motored over to Balcary Bay we manoeuvred the dinghy to avoid the sheets of ice as they floated out to sea in long lines. Along the coast road towards Auchencairn, the snow lay, with little drifts across the road, which we ploughed through, enjoying jolting and slipping through the snow. A farmer, driving in the opposite direction, waved to us vigorously, no doubt, he too was enjoying this unusually winter wonderland, and we waved cheerily back. As we came round the corner by the Seaside farm, we drove straight into a huge snow drift. The shelter of the woods had been left behind, and the snow had drifted off the fields and merse and piled up six feet high between the hedges on the road. The friendly wave from the farmer had been to warn us of what was to come. No doubt, he had just managed to dig himself out. Seaside farm was quite near, and soon a tractor came to our rescue to pull us clear of the drift. Unfortunately, it joined us by becoming stuck, and it took another tractor to drag us both clear of the drift. That was the end of our journey round to Colvend, and we drove back and garaged the van in the fish house.

As organist and Sunday School teacher, we were determined to reach Colvend. It was only Saturday, and we were spending the weekend at the manse, so we had plenty of time to find a way round. The snow crunched beneath our boots as we made our way down the lane, and then we skirted along the shore and struggled through the snow to Auchencairn, where the road had been cleared. About a mile out of the village, a milk truck gave us a lift to Palnackie. Palnackie is the next village above Kippford on the River Urr, but it is situated on the opposite side of the river, with the nearest crossing bridge at Dalbeattie. It wasn't too difficult trudging through the snow and down to the river bank at Glenisle, and we stood on the banks of Rough Firth, looking across to Kippford and blowing a whistle loud and long. We had phoned Fred from Auchencairn, and he was waiting with his dinghy to ferry us across. We had lunch with our friend, the session clerk, and later the minister came round and lifted us to Colvend in his car.

81

The journey back on Monday was also an adventure. Someone gave us a lift into Dalbeattie, and then we set off on the nine mile walk round to Balcary. Part way round, the coal man passed by, and offered us a lift to Auchencairn. We were quite prepared to walk from the village, but the coal merchant insisted on taking us to Balcary. The drifts had been snow-ploughed, but the road was still treacherous, and the lorry slid into the ditch. There was not much that we could do, except contact the farmer, who had pulled us out of the drift on Saturday. They were still struggling to drag the lorry out of the ditch when it was time for us to leave. The tide was coming in and we needed to walk over the flats and return to Heston before it was too late.

The unusual snow covering on Heston, also caused us trouble on the island. The byre that John had made weather proof for organ building, proved not to be snow proof. The blizzard had driven the snow through all the unsealed crevices, and about three inches of snow lay over all the polished wood work of the organ case, as well as covering the delicate mechanism. John was appalled, for weeks of work must surely be ruined. Fortunately, there had been a sharp frost before the snow, and everything was very cold, and the snow remained dry, enabling us to remove all of it without damaging the organ parts. During the winter months, Eddie worked on repairing his salmon nets. He had nets at Horse Isles as well as Balcary, and when he was working late and waiting for the tide to cover the rack, he sometimes anchored out in the shelter of the cliffs and came ashore in his dinghy to have a hot drink and a crack. "Crack" was the Galloway term for a good old natter with friends. We enjoyed these visits, it was good sitting round the glowing stove with the hiss of the Tilley lamp. When the tide had sufficiently covered the rack for Eddie's boat to clear it, we went down with him with the hurricane lamp to guide him passed the point. As Eddie waved to us that he was clear, we were aware that there was a scuffling around our feet. My first thought was that rats, which were numerous on the island, had come down to the shore; but no, we were amazed to see a flock of birds surrounding us, even running over our feet. We stood watching them and later discovered that they were purple sandpipers, they must have been attracted by the lamp. They were tightly clustered around our feet, and we stood perfectly still lest we hurt any of them. On looking them up in our book of birds, we discovered that purple sandpipers were winter visitors, but we had never seen any on Heston during the day time.

From a child I have always been interested in birds, but as a city dweller my knowledge was severely restricted. Heston was a revelation to me, especially in the winter. This was the time that ducks arrived to feed on the flats at the tide's edge. The widgeon were the most common visitors, and they came in their thousands, covering the sands like large black clouds, following the receding tide.

We could never get close to them, as soon as we were any where near they would all surge up into the sky and land a quarter of a mile away. Occasionally we would see a solitary duck that had left the flock, swimming near the shore, its distinctive chestnut and cream head contrasting with its grey body. There were black scoters, and a few goldeneyes near the shore with a white oval spot on the sides of their heads, and white under parts showing as they took off from the water. Each winter five loons took up residence in the currents off the point, their tremulous wailing cries filling the air with foreboding. They are the size of a goose, the long neck having distinctive glossy purplish black plumage, with a band of light stripes around the neck. The upper parts of these beautiful ocean birds are mottled with rows of white spots. They never leave the water except to breed. These, great northern divers, stirred my imagination, they had flown down to us leaving behind the desolate arctic wastes of the frozen north. When I was at school I was fascinated by the stories of arctic explorers, and for a while Robert Falcon Scott and his team were my heroes, and I read books on their calamitous but courageous trek to the south pole. I suppose my interest was aroused as my mother had book prizes from her days at school, that had been presented by Mrs. Oats. The school also possessed the flag that the men had taken with them to the south pole. Captain Oates had frost bite badly, and rather than hinder the others, he walked out into the blizzard one night to die. I loved to look at the pictures in a book that I had, painted by Edward Wilson who was one of the men who had been part of the expedition. He had a great Christian faith, and as a young Christian, he was a great inspiration to me.

It was fascinating trying to recognise the many birds on or around Heston. There were red-breasted mergansers to be seen all the year round. Guillemots could very occasionally be seen and I watched one in the current off the east cliffs, its little feet paddling vigorously to remain in the same place. I longed to see puffins, but although they used to breed, along with guillemots, in colonies on the Balcary heughs, there were none to be seen. Geese could be seen farther up the Solway on the merse. There is a bird sanctuary at Caerlaverock, not far from Dumfries, where the geese come in their thousands, much to the chagrin of the local farmers, for the geese did not heed any demarcation between the sanctuary and the near by farmer's fields. We only saw one flock of about fifty geese on Heston. They were smallish, and comparing them with pictures in the bird book, seemed to resemble Brent geese, but their colouring was more of a rich, dark green.

In a south-westerly gale the swell sweeps up the Solway unhindered, into the bay between Balcary and Heston. At high tide, when the water is deep, the waves sweep into the bay majestically, but at low tide the picture is quite different. In

83

shallow water the swell breaks into a mass of white, churning water. Returning to Heston at high tide on one January bitterly cold day, there was no wind, and the swell coming in from the open sea was unruffled. The dinghy rose gently up the mountain of glassy water and then slithered down into the trough, it was exhilarating, with an impressive view of the sea. By low tide a wind had come up, and the water in the bay was a seething mass of white topped waves breaking on the flats. As I watched the fascinating sight, I thought I could see two specks on the water about half a mile away, and ran to fetch the telescope for a better look. The specks were no longer visible and I wondered if they could have been men out on the water, and if so where were they now. It was unlikely that any one would venture out in the bay with the waves breaking and the water boiling. If it had been men they could be in trouble, but there was no way we could launch our dinghy and go to their aid, for it was coming up to low tide and we were at least a quarter of a mile from the edge of the sea. I called John, and we took it in turns to peer through the telescope, scanning the bay. Then we saw them, two men were in the water and were holding on to something. As we watched we could see that they were struggling through the water dragging a tiny water-logged dinghy, and along side them was a smaller figure. We hoped it was not a child, for the water is freezingly cold at this time of the year. As they came to shallower water we saw them try to tip up the boat, to empty out the water and re-float it, but the sea was far too rough and they continued dragging it to the shore. The small figure turned out to be a dog.

Early the next morning at low tide, an odd sight met my eyes, there were two men on the flats seemingly raking the mud. The telescope confirmed this, they had garden rakes and were in the middle of the wet sands, busily raking. The following day we walked off the island and met two men on the shore who asked us if we had seen any guns on the wet sands as we walked over. Obviously, these were the two men we had seen in the sea with the capsized dinghy, they had evidently been out duck shooting and disaster had struck. It was most unlikely that they would ever find their guns, for anything we had ever dropped into the sea just disappeared, the sea churning up the sand and mud and burying the object in its depths. Although, there was one occasion when a gleaming, chromium plated rowlock was dropped over board and could not be found at low tide, but it appeared about a year later. We told the men that we had witnessed their difficulties, but were unable to help them. They asked us not to mention what we had seen, especially to Eddie.

There was no need for us to keep quiet, for the next time we saw Eddie he told us the full story. The local policeman and hotel keeper from Auchencairn, where Eddie lived, had made themselves an eight foot dinghy to go duck shooting. They had proudly shown Eddie the boat and asked for his comments. He advised them strongly not to go out in the dinghy as it was not seaworthy, it was only suitable for fishing on a loch on a calm day. They took umbrage and were determined to show Eddie that he was wrong and had set out for an afternoon of duck shooting on the far side of the bay up Orchardton Lane, the river between Balcary and Heston. As soon as they came out of the shelter of the bay and hit the breakers the boat was swamped. The whole village soon knew the story, for the washing lines at both their houses were full of their wet clothes. There was much hilarity in the village over the episode, but the funniest part was an advert that appeared in the local paper. "For sale, small dinghy, suitable for loch fishing. Will take outboard motor" Their foolish adventure had evidently ended, not only in the loss of their guns, but had also ruined the outboard motor.

In the winter evenings we enjoyed reading, and had access to a good selection of books which we were allowed to borrow from Castle Douglas library. John went through a stage when he liked reading science fiction books. I am sure this was the cause of a mystery one evening when we were sitting in the window quietly reading by the gentle light of the oil lamp. Not long before John had been reading a book entitled "The truth about Flying Saucers." Down on the shore there was a strange white glow. I feel sure that the book had momentarily convinced John that flying saucers existed, and were often seen at lonely locations. What could be lonelier than Heston. The glow of light was strange and we had never noticed it before so we walked down to the beach to investigate. When we reached the spot there was nothing to be seen, had we imagined it? I think John was half expecting to see some little green men. Back in the cottage we peered out of the window and the glow was still there. We could not retire to bed until the mystery was solved, so once again we made our way down to the beach, but still no sign of the light. As you may have guessed, the solution was simple, and one we would have realised instantly, had we not been sole inhabitants of a lonely island, and let our imaginations run away with us. As we turned to make our way back to the cottage we caught sight of the Tilley lamp in the window, shining over the garden wall, its light hitting a patch of bleached shells on the shore, invisible in the light of the hurricane lamp.

Chapter 11 **Lighthouse and Engineers.**

"I am the light of the world. Whoever follows me will never walk in darkness but will have the light of life." (John ch. 8 v. 12.)

During that first winter on clear days, it was good to stand on the cliffs by the lighthouse and take in all the wonderful sights to be seen. Through my telescope I could see the English coast, about twenty miles away. On a very clear day it was even possible to distinguish buses, and imagine shapes which could be passengers boarding and leaving the vehicle. I could see fishing vessels working on the Solway, and even larger crafts, thirty miles away on the Irish Sea. In the cold weather sound travels well over the sea, and the chugging of engines could be heard from vessels many miles away. When the weather was quiet we could hear voices of those working on the mainland, and there have been times when I thought we must have visitors on the island, as the sound of voices was so clear.

We were often up at the lighthouse, for it had to be kept spotlessly clean, and the salt spray and seagull droppings soon dimmed the light. Ours was a minor light and operated automatically, using acetylene gas brought over in cylinders filled with acetone. The mechanism switched off the light during the day time to conserve the gas, since the cylinders were very heavy and difficult to transport. Some of the larger lighthouses situated on the coasts and rocks around Britain, no longer use lenses to magnify the light, but are rotating banks of electric spotlights. There are lightships guarding dangerous rocks and sand banks, buoy lights line the channels into the harbours, and numerous minor lights, like ours, scattered around the coasts to protect and guide shipping. The acetylene gas was very reliable and gave little trouble, but there was the danger of an explosion from the pressurised gas, and this together with the transporting difficulties, led the Lighthouse Authority to change the system again. After extensive trials, minor lights were changed from acetylene to propane gas, the cylinders being smaller and lighter. It was also a bonus that the empty cylinders could be handled very easily, since they were no longer filled with acetone as in the acetylene cylinders. The two engineers who would be responsible for the work would be with us for several days, and when notification of the change was sent to us we were asked to board the men. The mussel men brought Andrew McCurrach and Bob Naylor over from Kippford, and they slept in the second bedroom. In the event the change over did not give us such reliability as the old acetylene system. It seemed fine at first, but then we had problems, as propane was not as inflammable as acetylene it did not give such a strong flame, and blew out much more easily.   After our tenancy was over, the light was redesigned, and we are told that it is now much more reliable.

The engineers met a number of snags when they were installing the propane system, and the work took much longer than they had anticipated. This resulted in a domestic problem. I had catered with plenty of food for the time that they should have been with us, but the time was more than doubled. They were big men, with appetites much larger than ours. Normally, this would have been no problem, for we could either walk off or motor off the island and replenish our store of food. After their arrival a strong souwesterly gale blew up and this coincided with a neap tide. When the movement of the tides are small, the sea does not go out far, and in combination with a souwesterly gale the rack remains covered by the sea for several days, and it is impossible to walk off the island. It was also far too rough for our small dinghy. This happened while the engineers were with us, the fresh food ran out, and we were also getting low on other commodities. It was a case of making the available food last as long as possible. There was no problem with the dry provisions, for I always kept a large stock. We also had tinned food, but the engineers were not keen on this. Their job entailed travelling round the lighthouses, keeping them in good repair, as well as fitting new mechanisms. They had been caught out by gales many times and had had to exist on tinned food for days. Their pet hate was tinned pilchards, but they were safe from this, as I had none in the pantry. All the meat and fresh fruit and vegetables were finished, but I still had eggs and cheese. Bob smoked a pipe, and he ran out of tobacco, and paced the cottage. Andrew, jokingly, told me to lock up the tea caddy! We did get down to our last egg, yet I made it part of two meals for the four of us. Half was used to make a mayonnaise and mixed with the root vegetables still remaining. The other half was beaten into flour with dried milk and baking powder to make a thick batter and mixed with the left over cooked vegetables, this was made into fritters and fried.

The two men had a wealth of stories to recount, and we enjoyed their company. At night after the day's work was done, we sat round the roaring stove listening to Andrew and Bob tell tales of their roving lives, and the many hair raising adventures they had experienced while travelling round the Scottish lights. One of the lights they attended was the Skerries light, built on a rock low in the Pentland Firth. The current in the firth is unbelievable fast, and the Pentland Firth is one of the most treacherous waters in the world. Even quite big vessels can be driven backwards through those straits by the current. Many years ago the Orkney lifeboat was lost so tragically there. Andrew and Bob attended this light, travelling each day from the mainland in a motor boat. At the first sign of the tide turning it was essential for them to leave the Skerries and return quickly to the mainland. The men told us that the water rose like a wall which roared down the firth, sweeping everything before it. The skipper of the boat was a skilled seaman, with great experience of the firth, yet on one occasion he mis-judged the tide. The wall of water came rushing down and they only just man-aged to scramble into the boat, and using the full power of the motor and every-one pulling on the oars as hard as they could, they made the mainland three hours later, thankful to be alive.

Bob and Andrew had the difficult task of setting up a temporary light in the ruins of the Skerryvore lighthouse, situated on a rock ten miles south-west of Tiree. There had been a fire and the lighthouse was burnt out. The Skerryvore rocks are exposed to the full power of the Atlantic gales, and are on the regular shipping route round the north of Scotland. Yet, when the disaster occurred, the raging fire was not seen for three days, and the lighthouse keepers spent the time without shelter or food until they were rescued. Andrew and Bob landed on the rock and bunked below in the blackened ruin, while a third man, who had accompanied them to set up a radio link, set his equipment up on the third floor. The whole atmosphere was gloomy and eerie, but they climbed into their bunks that first night to get some sleep before starting the real work the next day. After awhile they were awoken by a tapping noise, as if someone was outside trying to get in. They checked that it was not the radio operator and went outside to see if there was any equipment that was loose, and could have caused the knock-ing. They were in the middle of the ocean, and certainly expected no visitors. Although they found nothing, the knocking still continued. These men were tough with nerves of steel but they could not help having bad thoughts. No one had ever found out how the fire had started, it was a mystery. Although on a busy shipping route, no one had seen the blazing inferno. Their fear, on that lonely rock in the middle of the ocean, began to get the better of them. Although by now it was the middle of the night they knew that they must subdue their fears before they could sleep, and the only way was to search the whole ruin. They were relieved when they found the cause. The temporary aerial had been installed well away from the wall, yet when the wind gusted in a certain direc-tion, it caused the aerial to oscillate and tap their window. They went back to bed laughing at themselves for behaving like frightened children, but a couple of hours later Andrew jumped out of his bunk shouting "Fire! We're on fire." Was this another bout of imagination, but no, black smoke was creeping down from above. The radio operator was sleeping peacefully, while his oil lamp had flared up, and the room was full of smoke. They went back to bed, but little sleep was had by either of them that night.

Skerryvore light is built on a rock lying in the approaches to the Minches chan-nel between the outer and inner Hebrides. The entrance door is high up on the tower and reached by an iron ladder. Stores are landed on the rock on a landing platform to which is attached a strong stanchion, where a cable from the ship can be attached as a hoist for unloading. When the lighthouse was rebuilt, a reinforced concrete block house was constructed on the rock to house some of the stores, instead of having to hoist everything up to the tower. Freak waves often hit the rock and one day Andrew was caught while on the landing platform and Bob was climbing up the ladder. As they saw the huge wave heading for them, there was no time to reach the tower entrance and Bob dropped from the ladder and hastily entered the concrete bunker bolting the door behind him. Andrew clung to the stanchion for dear life and hoped for the best. The water dragged him off his feet and as the wave passed he was left battered and bruised but still clinging on. The supposedly watertight bunker was half full of water when Bob escaped from it. On telling of their experiences to Bob's father-in-law, who was an islander and had served in the lighthouse service, the old man's verdict was that that reinforced block house would not last. The men argued that it would, for it was three feet thick and reinforced with steel; but the old man was right, within eighteen months it was smashed apart. It makes me wonder how any of these lighthouses built in such treacherous waters ever survive. They must be designed and built to withstand tremendous onslaughts of the sea.

After the men had left we were not happy with the new installation. It was much more unreliable and necessitated several hurried journeys back to Heston to re-light the lamp. If we were off for the weekend we often made several trips down to Rockcliffe shore to check on the light. One late trip was made not long after the wonderful auroral red skies, already described. Again, on returning from the bay, the curtains of green light were falling in the northern sky with shafts of brighter light shining through the ever moving display. We were staying at the manse, and brought the family out to watch the beauty of the canopy of the sky, as waves of greenish light made the sky alive. We sat up late that night and before going to bed, the minister went outside to have a last look at the night sky. He dashed back in, shouting to us to come outside quickly to see an amazing sight. The view that met us was breath taking. High above a huge star of silvery light glowed and from this great centre, pulsating beams of light cascaded down. The whole sky seemed to be filled with light. No longer was the light green as it had been earlier that night, or blanketed with a red glow, but shafts of light of many colours shimmered in the sky. From the silvery star the shafts of gold, crimson, scarlet, translucent green and deep blue, constantly changing pattern, filled the whole of the northern horizon. The light continuously changed, one colour dying down while another soared up to replace it. It was a magnificent sight, a vision of wonder that I have never seen before or since, but its unbelievable, ethereal beauty is something that I will never forget. In more recent years I have watched the 'Sound and Light' displays, and the coloured fountains played like music, but this does not compare with the beauty of the display of the northern lights on that intoxicating midnight long ago.

Chapter 12   Stories of Heston and Galloway from the past.

"For everything that was written in the past, was written to teach us." (Romans ch 15 v 4.)

I was interested in the history of Heston and its surroundings, and discovered a little of Heston's recent history. I knew that the previous tenants to Mr. Houston were the McWilliam family, and their daughter, May Maxwell, was named after the heroine in Crocket's "Raiders". The Tweedies occupied the island before the McWilliams, but there was a time when the island was uninhabited. The monks from Dundrennan Abbey, now a ruin several miles along the coast from Balcary, used to own the island. They are reputed to have made the two pools at the Balcary side of the rack. It is thought that the pools were constructed to catch salmon, but no one seems to know how they would work. Before the time of refrigeration, early in the medieval period, sea pools were constructed to keep the fish that had been caught fresh, or used to store lobsters, but as our pools would be covered by the sea when the tide was in, it seems unlikely that this was their purpose. We also heard a story that John Balliol, considered a traitor king by the Scots, built a palace on top of the island. There certainly are traces of a building up there, but it must have been a small palace, for the foundation stones occupy a negligible area.

One day Eddie brought two archaeologists over to look at the site, but they did not follow up their visit. I suppose they thought that it was not worth while coming over to dig out the ruins. Eddie said that if they had excavated, they would have found bones, for the story was that it was there that Tweedie had buried his horse. Eddie was a lovely man, but proud and would stand no nonsense or being made to look inferior. One of the archaeologists was very patronising and Eddie taught him a lesson on the sea trip back to the mainland. He suggested that they should go round the island to have a quick look at Copper Cove, where trial borings for copper had been made. His intention was to place the boat in such a position that on the way back this gentleman would receive the full force of the sea. Eddie apologised profusely for the rough ride back, which soaked this particular visitor well and truly, but felt his rebuffing had been avenged

One of the families who came sailing regularly from Kippford and often went fishing, caught a most unusual haul one day. Entangled in their net was an old mast. They left it on our island and it was covered with numerous growths of weed and wild life. It was obviously a mast off a schooner. The outcrops of rocks in the waters round Heston and the coast to the west, caused many a ship wreck. Just along the coast from Balcary is a memorial stone to the men who died when a Kippford built schooner was wrecked off the headland, many of those drowned were from Colvend. Perhaps, the mast fished out of the sea belonged to that wreck.

During the wars of independence, at the end of the thirteenth century and the fourteenth century, there were disputes as to the rightful king of Scotland. Among those put forward was John Balliol who was the senior surviving stem of the House of Canmore. To avert a civil war, King Edward of England was invited to settle the dispute. He was quick to take advantage of the situation, and tried to prove that he should have jurisdiction over the land, and demanded that his superiority should be recognised. Instead of being an arbitrator in the dispute he acted as the judge. John Balliol, who was a weakling, was chosen, and Edward demanded a humiliating dependence from Balliol. Balliol was expected to supply troops for the English side in the war against France, but the Scots refused, and broke away from England forming an alliance with France. In the ensuing battles with England, John Balliol was captured and taken to England. This was the beginning of the wars between England and Scotland which lasted over fifty years. Whether there was a connection between John Balliol and Heston, we were never able to prove, but he was certainly connected with the area. There is the remains of a castle ruin at Buittle, which is situated between Dalbeattie and Castle Douglas. The Balliol's lived there and probably built the castle. When we first drove up to Galloway we were impressed with the lovely scenery as we left Dumfries behind and began the journey along the coast road. New Abbey is a small village on the route and its main attraction is the remains of Sweetheart Abbey. It is well situated with a beautiful backdrop provided by Criffel, a steep hill whose slopes are covered with moorland and woodland. John Balliol's wife Devorgilla was very much in love with her husband, and was devastated when he died. She had his heart embalmed and encased in a silver casket and carried it about with her. She left plans for an Abbey to be built, as a memorial for her husband and her body and the casket were buried in the foundations. She also endowed Balliol College, Oxford, which had been established by her husband.

Returning, in reflection, to Sweetheart Abbey, reminds me of a visit made there in the early nineteen sixties. We had adopted our first baby, and during the visit we had tea in New Abbey at a lovely old tea shop. The baby was old enough to sit in a high chair to enjoy his milk. On the table, far too near to Stephen, was a bright shining silver teapot. He was mesmerised by the radiant pot and wanted to touch it. I made it quite clear to him that it was very hot and would hurt him, and he must not touch it. He was determined to touch that pot, and in a second when I was distracted, he put out his hand and felt it. Even at that age, less than a year old, he knew he had done wrong. Instead of crying, as was the norm when he hurt himself, he withdrew his hand and held it without a murmur. When I managed to pry his fingers open, they were blistered from the burn and must have been painful. Whatever our age, we have an in-built knowledge of right and wrong, together with a spiritual need. In this post modern age religion is often denigrated, yet at times of disaster people instinctively turn to God for help.

Dumfries is an ancient town, although there is little left of the medieval part. It was very important, and in the twelfth century became a royal burgh. Devorgilla's Bridge over the River Nith is at the site where Devorgilla had a timber bridge built over the Nith, and this was probably in the thirteenth century. The River Nith flows through the modern town, and this old fifteenth century, red sandstone bridge, was once the entrance to the town with a toll house at the far end. At one time the River Nith was navigable and the villages along its banks were busy ports trading with many foreign parts. Kingholm and Glencaple were busy ports in the eighteenth and nineteenth century, their trade stretching out to the West Indies, North America and the Baltic. Glencaple is noted as a place where the 'bore' can be seen at certain times. When the combination of tide and wind are right, a wall of water, one or two feet high, rushes up the River Nith, and is quite spectacular. The lighthouse at Southerness was built by the Dumfries merchants in the eighteenth century. Dumfries was often burned and plundered during the border raids between the English and the Scots. There is little left of that period in Dumfries except the ruined remains of Lincluden College, which was once the site of a rich monastery and was a place that Burns loved and wrote about. Robert Bruce is associated with Dumfries at Greyfriars Monastery, which is long gone. One of his followers stabbed to death the Red Comyn, who was one of the claimants for the throne. This enabled Bruce to reign and led eventually to the defeat of the English. Near to Dumfries is the remains of Caerlaverock Castle. Caerlaverock is now a Wildfowl Refuge, and thousands of Barnacle geese descend there each winter, and it is one of the important places in Britain for wildfowl and wading birds.

Dumfries and the south-west of Scotland were centres of the Covenantors in the seventeenth century. This was a time of compulsory church attendance and puritanical living. There were many witch hunts and nine women were burnt at the stake at Whitesands, which is now a huge car park. There are memorials to Robert Burns in the town, for he spent the last five years of his life there. Along the road leading from the village of Bankend, a well can be found, where it is said Robert Burns bathed in the hope of a cure for his illness. One of our exploratory days out took us to Ruthwell where we could see the famous,

93

ancient celtic cross, which is now housed inside the church. The cross is beautifully carved, and dates from the end of the seventh century. Figures from the Gospels are carved, along with decorations and Latin inscriptions from the Vulgate Bible. At the edges runes, a form of ancient writings, have been deciphered and found to record a sacred poem. Ruthwell also celebrates being the first village to have a parish bank. There is a Trustees Saving Bank museum in the village.

Dalbeattie, the nearest town from Kippford, is noted for its granite. Quarrymen came up from Mount Sorrel in Leicestershire to work in cutting and polishing this very fine granite. Most of the Dalbeattie houses built in the nineteenth century are of grey granite. The quarrymen wanted to worship in the Anglican tradition, and built themselves a beautiful, granite church in the town. Christ Church is a Scottish Episcopalian Church and is very beautiful. Some of the present members are the offspring from those Leicestershire quarrymen. Vast amounts of granite were shipped out from Dalbeattie all over the world, and some were used in the Embankment in London, in New York and other important sites. Kippford, as well as a fishing village, also built two masted schooners in the nineteenth century. The village of Palnackie was an important port for exporting slates, coal and timber, and in the seventeenth century exported millstones. The whole of the coast west of Heston was noted for smuggling activities. The hotel at Balcary was one of the old haunts of smugglers, used for shelter and as a hide-out. Inland from the coast cattle smuggling was rife.

Dundrennan Abbey, once owners of Heston, was built in the twelfth century and was a great Cistercian monastery. Dundrennan has a connection with the Catholic queen, Mary Queen of Scots. Mary returned from France to Scotland at the time when Catholicism was denounced as idolatrous, and many of the abbeys and monasteries were destroyed. The authority of the Pope was abolished and the celebration of mass forbidden. Mary received the full force of the diatribes of John Knox. After her disastrous marriages and suspicion of her complicity in the death of her husband Darnley, she lost much of her support from the people, and fled to Dundrennan. It was from there that she crossed the Solway by boat and sought help in England from Queen Elizabeth. She then spent the rest of her life in prison in England, so her last night on Scottish soil was spent at Dundrennan. The Cistercian monks were noted for their way of life, work being an important part of prayer. The Abbey became rich through the wool trade, and the local people worked for the monks looking after the sheep. There is an unusual round tower, Orchardton Tower, not far from Heston, built in the area between Auchencairn and the Almorness Peninsular, and it is unique in Scotland. These fortified towers, called peles, were built with stone to withstand fire and siege, and were homes as well as fortresses, and places of refuge in the times of the border raids. Before castles were built with stone, wooden buildings were built on earth mounds and protected by deep ditches. Remains of these motes can be found at the Mote of Urr, just outside Dalbeattie, and the Mote of Mark at Rockcliffe.

The area of Galloway and around Dumfries has associations with many famous people. Thomas Telford was born in Eskdale, the bridge over the River Dee at Tongland, which is now noted for the hydroelectric scheme, was designed by him. Paul Jones, the founder of the United States navy, left his home in Arbigland to go to America, after being involved in a brawl and fleeing from justice. With his knowledge of sailing, he then returned in charge of an American ship and raided the coasts of England, including the Solway. As well as the association of Robert Burns with the area, there were other authors, including Sir Walter Scott, who often visited the area and set his book 'Guy Mannering' near Dumfries. J. M. Barrie went to school in Dumfries, and John Buchan set part of his Thirty-nine Steps' around Cairnsmore of Fleet. Similarly the authors Dorothy Sayers and Gavin Maxwell wrote about, or were associated with, the region.

The west part of the region is one of the cradles of Christianity in Britain. St. Ninian came to the country by sea and founded the first Christian church at Whithorn in the early part of the fifth century, although it is thought that there were small pockets of Christians in the area even before this time. Ninian was the son of a converted chieftain of the Cumbrian Britons, and went as a youth to Rome, where he was instructed in the faith. After being consecrated Bishop in 394, probably by Pope Siricius, he set out to convert Scotland. On his journey through Tours he made the acquaintance of St. Martin, and dedicated the church he founded in Whithorn to him. This church, called Candida Casa (White House) probably on account of the colour of the stones, became a centre for Ninian's work. From this site in Wigtownshire Ninian and his monks conducted a mission to the neighbouring Britons and the Picts. In the Middle Ages Ninian's tomb in the church was a favourite shrine of pilgrimage. The site has been excavated, and today there is a museum and centre at Whithorn, giving the history of Ninian. There is also a cave which Ninian is reputed to have used.

Less civilised are the members of the Sawney Bean family who lived in a cave in a remote area of the country. The people of that region were growing increasingly worried by the number of people, especially travellers, who disappeared regularly. The story goes that one day a couple were attacked by a gang of wild people, and their lives were only saved by a group of travellers returning that way from a fair. The attackers were followed to their cave, and soldiers were sent out to investigate the family. A gruesome sight met the eyes of the soldiers, the cave was a veritable butchers shop, but the joints hanging up and the meat pickled in brine were those of human beings. The family of cannibals were led away and executed.

The nearest town from Balcary is Castle Douglas. This is a town that was built in the late eighteenth century by Sir William Douglas. He had made a fortune as a merchant in Virginia and the West Indies, and spent money in establishing a commercial centre in his native Galloway. His original idea of establishing the town as a centre for the cotton industry failed, but instead it became famous for cattle and horse fairs. It is still one of the most modern auction markets in Scotland. Situated by the town is Carlinwalk Loch, and when it is frozen over in the winter, it is popular for playing curling. At the end of the loch are the beautiful gardens of Threave. The ruins of Threave Castle can be seen on an island in the River Dee and can be reached by ferry.

Chapter 13. **New Horizons.**

"By the new and living way that he opened for us." (Hebrews ch. 10 v. 20.)

Our money situation made it imperative that we make the organ business pay. We could only grow a small proportion of our food, due to the tenancy restrictions. In the second year our skill at fishing failed us, or the codling had left our waters, for day after day the lines were baited, but there were no fish. Our outgoings were small, only twenty five pounds a year for rent, and a few pounds for rates, but our total income of one hundred and eighty pounds a year was not sufficient for even our basic needs. The money we had set aside to assist us financially, while we were building up the business, had now been used up in buying the equipment, wood etc. for building the first organ. There was still five hundred pounds safe in a building society, although it had earned no interest. We were lucky that we had not lost all our savings in the bankruptcy, and thankful that another building society had taken over. We were determined not to touch this, as we knew that we would need the money to provide a deposit for a house, when our three year contract was over.

In our second spring we hit rock bottom money wise. We were off the island to make arrangements for the sheep to leave Heston at the end of May. We arranged for the farmer to come over to Heston for the sheep in about three weeks time. We would then receive the fifty pound cheque, and our financial dilemma would be eased. Meanwhile we were hard pressed even to scrape enough money together to buy our weekly groceries. The crisis was an immediate one, even if we had decided to withdraw some of the house money, it would need notice time before it became available to us. As we left the farm house and were walking down towards the van, David, the farmer called us back. "I might as well give you the cheque now" he said. "It will save me remembering to bring the cheque book when I come over in three weeks time." Thankfully we received the cheque, cashed it, no waiting time in those days, and were able to buy the groceries. Once again God had provided for us. It is good to look back over life and see how our needs have been provided and to give thanks for the bountiful provision and gifts of love from our heavenly Father.

I made good use of all the food we grew, and wasted none, even eating lettuce and rhubarb for breakfast on occasions, when we had a glut of this produce. Cooking lettuce as a vegetable had not proved appetizing, and we had no way of preserving it, but, together with the other vegetables we grew we ate healthily. One day as I was wandering at the south end of the island, I made a wonderful find. There was a patch of mushrooms growing. I hastily gathered them up and carried them home, they weighed just over three pounds. We both loved mushrooms, especially fried, served on toast with the juices made into a thick sauce. The rest I made into mushroom soup, which was bottled. In those days few people had refrigerators or deep freezers; these commodities were luxuries possessed by the better off, even on the mainland where there was electricity. Food was preserved by bottling, or in some cases by being layered in salt, a method used to preserve runner beans.

Gull eggs again proved a useful source of protein. Thinking about gulls eggs reminds me of an incident that happened on Rough Island. This island is a bird sanctuary and is just off the coast at Rough Firth, between Rockcliffe and Kippford. It is popular with visitors, for it is possible to walk over to it at low tide. One of the attractions is a large rock called the 'camel rock', it really does look like a camel. We have a rock attraction on Heston, too, the 'elephant rock', again it really does resemble an elephant with its trunk, when viewed from a certain angle. To return to the egg story. The Dutch coasters that regularly came up to Palnackie were often family boats, with the skippers wife and family aboard, living in neat, curtained cabins. If they had missed the tide or wanted to have a weekend off, they beached the vessel on the flat sands by Rough Island. The crew from one of these boats had enjoyed themselves by raiding the nests on the island and taking off many of the eggs. These are, of course, protected, and the local bird watchers were very angry and made protests to the authorities. Apparently, official protests were sent to the Dutch government, who took a very serious view of the matter, and the skipper and his crew were in deep trouble. It seems that the fact of the sandwich terns nesting on Heston during our first spring was due to this disturbance, as normally they nested on Rough Island.

The organ business began to grow once our first pipe organ was installed. We also started to build up an organ tuning round. Although we were still thoroughly enjoying island life, it was becoming more and more necessary to make trips to the mainland to secure orders and carry out the work. On many occasions we experienced difficulties leaving Heston, due to the weather and tides, and our times on the mainland were often unsociable hours. We decided to look for a small cottage that could be used as a mainland base. This would also be good for the transition from island to mainland, when our three year tenancy was over. Originally we had hoped to buy the island, but the owners would not sell since owning an island was seen as very prestigious. It would not have been a good investment, for the cottage and out buildings were in a poor state with wood worm and dry rot. It would have needed a fortune to put everything in order. Then there was the problem of children. One of our plans was to have two children, this had not happened, but we still hoped that we would have children eventually. As far as we know, only one child had lived on Heston, May Maxwell McWilliam, and when she was old enough to go to school she went to live with her grandmother in Auchencairn. When we had children we had no intention of leaving them for some one else to rear, whether by a relative or at a boarding school.

At that time in Scotland there were no specialised house selling agents, houses were sold by solicitors. We paid a visit to our solicitor in Dalbeattie and learned that a cottage had come on to the market that day, and was already vacant. It was situated next to Colliston Park in Dalbeattie, and had two bedrooms and two sitting rooms. There was an attached lean-to that housed the kitchen and bathroom, although its entrance was outside the main building. We went to view the property, liked it, and made an offer for it of five hundred pounds, the amount we had in the building society. The owner worked for the South of Scotland Electricity Board and our solicitor was able to contact him. He came round to the solicitor's, agreed to the sale, and we were given the keys that very same day and took possession of the cottage before returning to Heston. Since that time I have been involved in selling and buying houses on many occasions, but never have experienced such swift proceedings.

Our cottage was called Islecroft, named because the land on which it was built was bounded by the burn on one side and a mill lade on the other. This island was about the same acreage as Heston and built on it were two cottages, an old, disused flour mill higher up the mill lade, and a sawmill next door to our cottage. At that time the sawmill still used water power to drive its machinery. Our present age is very safety conscious, and I am sure the authorities nowadays would be horrified to see the saw, uncovered and easily accessible to children playing in the park. There seemed to be no safety guards, the timbers pushed through the saw by hand. The main water way flowing through the centre of Dalbeattie passed behind our cottage, and we could take a short cut to the main shopping street by crossing the burn on huge stepping stones. When the burn was in flood the stepping stones were covered, and it was impassable, and we had to walk round the roads to get to the shopping area. The huge boulders that formed the stepping stones were slippery and difficult to cross when the water was high, but presented a great challenge. As you can imagine, they were a great attraction to children, and in our short stay at Islecroft, I have dried out many a child. Today, the burn is crossed by a stout bridge, and the fun of crossing over the stepping stones is a thing of the past.

It was lovely having the beautiful Colliston Park on our doorstep, complete with a large pool, fed by the burn. While we were there a pair of swans nested each year on an island at the centre of the pool. Every year they hatched four eggs, three producing the usual tawny coloured cygnets, but the fourth was pure white. The parents would not accept the white cygnet and attacked it, shortly after it was hatched. Every one kept a watch on the nest, and at the first sign of hatching the R.S.P.B. were notified. They came down to the park straight way to rescue the unfortunate white offspring, who would otherwise have been killed. The cottage proved to be ideal for our use. We could use one of the sitting rooms to store tools and finished parts of organs. Having electricity meant that it would be far easier to test the electrical equipment. At first we camped out in the cottage, the sleeping bags and utensils from our camping holidays coming in very useful. As we started to earn money from the business we were able to furnish the cottage with second-hand furniture and buy electric tools to help with the cabinet work. The work of organist and Sunday School teacher also became simpler. Although our friends at the manse were very hospitable and assured us that they loved having us at the weekend, we felt that we were imposing on them, and were happier that we had a place of our own.

Our island duties were still carried out and we enjoyed the respite and solitude of Heston after our mainland work. The evenings were spent quietly sitting in the comfort of the glowing stove and hissing lamp, and we had time to plan the business. We also planned our dream house, although we thought it would be a number of years before we could afford to build a house on the coast. In the event we were wrong, our new house plans came to fruition much earlier than we had ever thought possible.

In that second summer we continued to revel in island life. There were no rabbits on Heston, many years earlier a number of weasels had made their way over to Heston, I suppose they had come over the rack from the Almorness peninsular. During their stay, they cleared out every rabbit from the island. Whether the rabbits have since returned, I do not know, but there were no rabbits there in our time. I have always been interested in wild life, and this interest grew during our stay on the island. I was thrilled on one occasion to see a school of porpoises moving down the firth on their way to the sea. The local people told us that porpoises were usually seen before a gale blew up. There must have been about fifty travelling in groups of about three. It was wonderful seeing them move slowly through the water in a typical, gambolling fashion, and listen to their snuffling noises. I also saw a lone creature, one day in June, swimming up and down the beach below the cottage. Earlier there had been a shoal of small fish in the same place. The dark shape was clearly visible below the water, but whether it was a porpoise or a small basking shark, I do not know. There were all kinds of marine animals washed up on the Heston shore, especially large jelly fish, to which we gave a wide birth, for they had stingers. Small octopus were often seen and sea anemone. The water was full of plankton, one celled plants and animals which were the basic nutrition of the food chain. Some of these minute creatures were phosphorescent. We discovered this one night when we were walking back to the island over the wet sands. As we walked fluorescent green sparks flew up from our feet. We went out on the sea in the dinghy and the bow sliced through the water leaving a green glow, while behind us the outboard motor churned up the sea and left in its wake a brilliant path of green light. As we dipped the oars and lifted them out of the water droplets of light fell back into the sea. We even went swimming in the sea on one of the phosphorescent periods, and it was wonderful being surrounded by a green glow as we splashed in the water. The flashes of light only occurred when the minute animals were disturbed by vibrations. It seems that the appearance of phosphorescence in the sea also preceded a southerly gale.

We often needed to walk on and off the island when the weather and tides were unsuitable for the dinghy. There always seemed to be heavy loads to carry, either shopping, or tools and organ parts. To help with carrying heavy loads, we started to use our two-wheeled pig barrow, although this could be difficult when the lane was deep. It necessitated unloading the bags of goods and transporting the barrow over the water before reloading. Mr. Houston told us that his furniture came over to Heston by horse and cart, and the cart became bogged down in the lane and caused the loss of some of his furniture. It would have been quicker and simpler to cross the lane lower down, but our one attempt at this was a sharp warning, and caused us to steer clear of these quick sands. One of the previous tenants had tried to bring his horse and cart over to Heston the short way, and his horse had sunk into the quick sands and had only been rescued after tremendous efforts. Another story told to us concerned two mainland farmers who had come over to Heston to buy calves. They ignored local advice and drove a car over, since the sands appeared to be firm, and became stuck in the lane. They were unable to recover the car before the tide came in, and after the sea had covered it for a night, it became a complete write-off.

The tide often washed up flotsam which had probably fallen over board from ships ploughing through storms. As already recounted, during the war Eddie was lucky enough to find a barrel of lard washed up on the shore. For many years John used lubricating oil for his boat engines from a barrel of oil that was washed up on Heston. His good, substantial workbench was made from planks of wood, sixteen feet long and two inches thick, timber that had fallen off a Canadian timber vessel. The wood had washed up in Copper Cove and was very difficult to manoeuvre up the cliff path round to the cottage. It was well worth the effort, and after John died, ten years ago, my son transported it for his own workshop, as it was still in excellent condition. One gruesome find on Heston, fortunately not by us, was a body from a sailing accident that happened while we were on the mainland.

In the summer months we sat on the cliff top watching the yachts racing from Kippford. The smaller racing dinghies sailed round Rough Island, but we had an excellent view of the larger yachts that ventured out into the rough waters around Heston. The 'F' buoy was below the cliffs and the big keel yachts heeled over gracefully as they rounded the buoy before sailing back. Kippford Yacht Club was well known and its members travelled all over the country taking part in races. In the days when the schooners used to load up in Kippford, there was a rail track running down from a granite quarry in the hills above Kippford. When the granite was worked out, the old track which came down the hill and across the road to the jetty, was no longer needed. The rails were taken up for scrap during the war, but the old jetty remained. The yacht club bought the jetty and built a launching ramp and a dinghy park around it, and a club house. Every year there was a regatta and many sailors brought their yachts from afar. There was great excitement at the opening as Uffa Fox, the designer of the Flying Fifteen, brought Prince Philip's boat, "Cowslip", to Kippford for the official opening. After the ceremony, he sailed in "Cowslip" in a special commemorative race. While we were living on Heston the first catamarans arrived in Kippford. They were the sixteen foot long Shearwater III, with their distinctively battened sails. The speed they cut through the water was thrilling. They sailed long distances, often across to England or over to the Isle of Man. They covered the distance of about forty miles, to Whitehaven in Cumberland and back, at an average speed of twenty miles an hour. There was a great disadvantage with catamarans, once they started to capsize, they were very difficult to control, and even more difficult to retrieve once capsized. Later we owned a twenty six foot catamaran, and were always very careful to sail within its limits, we had learned a lesson by watching the Kippford catamarans in trouble.

During our second summer our visitors spent part of their holiday with us at Islecroft, as well as enjoying a spell on the island. John's parents came up with an aunt and uncle. It was a busy time for John as he had an organ to install. John's father was a very practical man and always ready to help. Instead of coming over to Heston he offered to go with John and help to install the organ. I set out with the two ladies and John's uncle. Unfortunately, as we set off over the flats a thick sea mist came down and blotted out the distant landmarks, but I had a compass and we were never in any danger. My mother in law was a very nervous lady, and no doubt was wishing that her practical son and husband were leading the party over to Heston. She will never be forgiven by John's uncle, when she plaintively remarked that she was very worried having no man in the party! As well as the mist rain set in, and we all arrived in a bedraggled state. It was easy finding dry clothes for the ladies, but Uncle Tom had to make do with one of John's kilts. He was the subject of much mirth, but really enjoyed the experience. The walk and the island air gave them all a large appetite, especially Uncle Tom, and my home made bread and cakes disappeared rapidly.

Chapter 14 **Bidding Farewell.**

"Finally, brothers and sisters, farewell, put things in order." *(2 Corinthians ch. 13 v. 11)*

The three year tenancy was soon up, and it was time to return fully to the mainland. We had enjoyed a wonderful three years, and the experiences, good and bad will always be part of my life. It was a high light in my journey through life, and I look back on that time with nostalgia, but life does not exist solely on high lights, but must be well balanced. That time was not just an adventure, an exciting interlude, but a constructive time of much learning. During those first two years, we realised that with the limitations of the tenancy, it would be very difficult to make a proper living from Heston, and even more difficult to bring up a family there. If we had had an endless supply of money I suppose we could have built a paradise on the island. It would probably have been possible to build a harbour and enabled us to moor a large boat which could cope with all weathers. A modern house powered by generated electricity would make life easier. However, even if we had had a bottomless pit of money, that would not be the Heston that we had come to love. Lives, both physical and spiritual, thrive on hard work and difficulties, and appreciating God's wonderful natural creation.

By the time the lease was up our business was going well and we needed to expand. It would have been unwise to renew the tenancy. We already had a base at Islecroft in the town of Dalbeattie, so the transition was made easy. In the eighteen months that we had owned the cottage we had greatly improved it. A conservatory had been built on to join the kitchen and bathroom to the rest of the cottage. Many improvements were made, including installing a hot water system. John's father came up and helped us with the brick laying and plumbing, and the work was done at minimum expense. The cottage was very old, several hundred years it seemed, perhaps five hundred. No one knew what had become of the deeds, they had been missing as long as any one could remember. The cottage was not large enough to accommodate us and the business, so we needed to rent a workshop, and began looking for a suitable building. The old flour mill was just a few hundred yards from us, and we were lucky enough to rent it. It was very old and needed to be treated for wood worm, for we did not want our organs to become infected. The cottage and old mill were duly prepared so that we would have a straight forward removal. As it became necessary to spend more and more time on the mainland, in those last few months, we made sure that our island duties were not neglected. It was a seven mile journey down to Rockcliffe, where we knew that we could check the lighthouse each night. To avoid this expense, both in money and time, we decided to look for a nearer viewing point, if one existed. The highest point in Dalbeattie should enable us to see the light, and finally we discovered that it could be seen from the top end of Dalbeattie cemetery, and this was only a ten minute walk away from the cottage. Our trips up to the cemetery, on the nights we were spending at Islecroft, were often quite eerie, especially as the tomb stones echoed our foot fall as we walked up to the far corner.

When we were exploring this area above Dalbeattie we found the Rounall Wood. At one time this had been part of a large estate, and although now neglected, it had once been well cared for and a beautiful place. John's parents were staying with us when we discovered the woods. We had just returned from taking them over to the Isle of Arran for a holiday. It was a working holiday for us, as we were carrying out preliminary work on an order for an organ at Corrie church, in a village along the coast from Brodick. There was a spectacular show of wonderful rhododendrons in Brodick castle gardens which we had visited, and we were all very impressed with the number of different varieties and the beautiful variegated colours of the large flowers. On our exploration outing through the Rounall Woods, we discovered a similar, beautiful selection of rhododendron varieties, almost equal to those at Brodick Castle. This was the first time that we had ventured in this area and it was a wonderful discovery. Probably many of the inhabitants of Dalbeattie were unaware of their existence. The Rounall Wood is now well cared for, with paths, seats and a picnic area.

Eddie was taking over the tenancy of Heston, and had the contract for looking after the lighthouse. He intended to use the cottage for holiday makers. As we had bought extra furniture for Islecroft, we were able to leave some of the furniture and fittings on Heston to get him started. The removal was carried out by ourselves, using the boat and van, and we were able to spread the work over several weeks in between our organ commitments. When it came to transporting the larger pieces of furniture, we were surprised how much more the dinghy held compared with the van. On one occasion we had loaded the three piece suite easily into the boat, but however hard we tried, the van would not accommodate the last armchair. We did not want to have to drive all the way back just for one chair, so we tied it securely to the roof of the van. Eddie had been helping us to load, and asked if we could give him a lift back into the village. You can guess which was the only available space for Eddie. He climbed up onto the top of the van and sat in comfort in the armchair. As we approached the village, much to our alarm, the local policeman was coming in the opposite direction on his bicycle. Eddie shouted a greeting to him and waved, and the policeman waved happily back. The law was much more laid-back and friendly in those days, especially in the country.

On our last official day as tenants of Heston, we arranged the Southwick Sunday School outing to sail round the island in Eddie's boat. There were about a dozen children, I think every child living in the wee village and surrounding farms came on the trip. The children were taken round to Balcary in our van and the minister's car, stopping on the way at the Auchencairn village store for the children to stock up with sweets, crisps, ice-cream and pop. There was a swell on the sea and we wondered if we would regret stopping at the shop, but we need not have worried. The children were carried aboard and we sailed round the island before landing on the beautiful golden sands of Whiteport Bay. Everyone had a great time, although several of the children had to be wrung out. They loved paddling in the sea and getting soaked as the waves broke on the shore. One of the young children was fascinated by the foamy water churned up by the engine and spent the whole of the trip back hanging over the side, with me clinging to her legs. It was a lovely way to spend our last day, enjoying fun with the children.

While we were on Heston we had spent many cosy evenings planning our dream house. We wanted a large sitting room with full height so that we could build a pipe organ in the room, and also have a large stain glass window at one end. The plan had open stairs leading to a mezzanine floor, where the organ would be built, which would also give access to the bedrooms. In his apprenticeship, John had studied draftmanship, which came in very useful for planning and technical drawings for the organs. He now put his skills to drawing the plans for our dream house. The business was going well and we reckoned that perhaps in five or six years we could afford to build it. In the event, we built our house at Kippford, and moved into our new home in just over a year from the time we left Heston.

Chapter 15. The Mainland and more Dreams Fulfilled.

"The joyous mother of children." (Psalm 113 v. 9.)

Although we were sad to leave behind our island life, we were very busy fulfilling the obligations of our new business. As a young person I had vowed that I would never work in an office, but I found myself typing letters, costing materials, sending out quotations etc. Since it was our own business I had an incentive to do this work. In addition I would accompany John on visits to potential customers and also learned to do some of the physical work in our new workshop. Having small hands, I found that I was very good at doing some of the intricate work, such as making small leather motors to operate the organ mechanism, and wiring up the many electrical connections that were needed in a pipe organ that was operated electrically. The heavy cabinet work I left to John, although I came in useful by holding on to pieces of woodwork which required more than one pair of hands. In those early days we worked long hours each day for six days a week, Sunday only was our day off, which we devoted to our spiritual needs. When we moved to Scotland we became members of the kirk, the Church of Scotland, which was the only church within reasonable distance. Soon we were involved in church work, John as organist, and I took over the Southwick Sunday School. We had belonged to a Baptist Church before moving to Scotland, which had regular holy communion services. In the fifties and early sixties, many of the kirks only celebrated the communion, partaking of the bread and wine, once or twice a year. Taking communion every week was very important to us and we had missed it. This was the one service that Jesus had instituted and the early disciples met weekly in each others houses to partake of the Lord's supper.

One of the organs which we restored was in the Episcopal Church in Ellon. In those days Ellon was a quiet, small town, but since the arrival of oil in the east of Scotland, it is now a thriving, busy oil town. The Scottish Episcopal Church was unknown to us, but while we were in Ellon we were invited to attend the morning service. Rules and regulations regarding the taking of bread and wine in different denominations were then very strict. Only confirmed members of an Anglican church were allowed to take part in the communion, and as we were not members we were not allowed to partake. It was very sad that these restrictions existed and prevented us from joining fully in the service. Over lunch we discussed this with the rector telling him of our concern that we rarely received bread and wine because of the infrequency of the communion service in the kirk. The rector found a loop hole in the regulations, and the following Sunday we were allowed to share fully in the service. This was a wonderful experience for us, for we had so missed taking communion, and the service was made even more joyful for us by the lovely music settings of the liturgy. Both John and I enjoyed singing and music, and we were thrilled that we had found a church that fulfilled our needs, both in weekly communion and in a rich diet of beautiful music.

Just as that wet holiday in the second year we visited Scotland, resulted in our island dream being fulfilled, so this introduction to the Scottish Episcopal Church was the means of further dreams being fulfilled. We were put in touch with the rector of the Dalbeattie church, and this lead to our becoming members of Christ Church, Dalbeattie. We were very happy to continue our work in the Colvend churches, since we could enjoy a Communion Service at half past eight and a beautiful Evensong at six o'clock. Neither interfered with our morning services at the kirk, for these were at eleven and twelve o'clock. However, this did not work out, the kirk insisting that we choose one or the other, we were not allowed to attend both. In those days there was little ecumenicalism, and little love lost between the kirk and the Episcopal church. Thankfully, things have changed for the better over the years, and many churches are willing to have ecumenical services and co-operate in the work of the church. We joined the Episcopal church fully, and John became their organist. The church also ordered one of our organs, the smallest model, which in those days cost £250. This one manual pipe organ is still used regularly although it was built over forty years ago.

As a result of our working very long hours we built the business up quickly. This resulted in being able to afford to build the house, that we had planned in the cosy evenings on Heston, much sooner than we had ever imagined. There was a plot of land, about half an acre in area, half way down the main road into the village of Kippford. Enquiries were made about the land and we were told by the locals, and eventually our solicitor, that building was not allowed there. It was sandwiched between a bungalow, belonging to one of the mussel men, and a large house just above. There was no sewage system in the village at that time, and houses used septic tanks and the over-spill found its way into the burn, which flowed down the side of the road passing near to all the houses. This decree had been passed many years before. On investigation, we found that several years earlier the burn had been diverted across the land that we hoped to buy, and therefore, any effluent from the new house would not enter the remains of the burn which still flowed beside the road. There was no longer any health hazard to the houses below. No one had noticed this, or wondered why the burn was now just a small trickle. Our solicitor was interested in our story, and came down to examine the plot of land for himself. Our observations were correct and we were able to buy the land and build our house. After we were living in Kippford, quite a number of people asked us how we had obtained permission to build, when others had been turned down.

The bank manager was very helpful and suggested that it would be advantageous for us to borrow the money we needed as a bank loan instead of a mortgage. Over the past few years we had become used to being frugal, and very little money had been spent on luxuries. This method of financing the house was the right one for us, and we were able to pay off the loan in a much shorter time than a mortgage at a fixed rate. The house was built according to our plans, but first of all we needed to clear the site which was covered with a forest of brambles, over eight feet tall, entwined with bushes and numerous weeds. It was a great thrill when the clearing was finished and the building begun. The house was built by the local Dalbeattie builder. The moving in was memorable. We had sold our cottage in Dalbeattie and given them a fixed day for entry. As is usual when building a house there were delays, this time with the firm supplying the flooring, and the new house was not completed on time. I clearly remember our first night in Alderburn. The house was complete except for the laying of tiles throughout the down stairs area. We had promised the cottage key to the buyers and could not go back on our contract. We moved as much furniture as possible to the finished upstairs area, storing the rest in the old Dalbeattie workshop. The tile layers also had a contract with our builders, and in order to avoid penalties, worked overtime to complete the work before morning. As we climbed into bed upstairs, we could hear the sound of a loud gas blower melting tar in which the tiles were laid. By the morning they had finished and avoided a fine. Clearing the land at the front of the house was completed, but the rear was covered by a small wood of alder trees, through which the burn flowed; hence the name Alderburn. There was plenty of land and eventually we built a new organ studio in the grounds, which proved to be much more convenient than travelling to the old mill workshop each day.

The tenth anniversary of our wedding had been celebrated by the time we moved into our Kippford home. As the business gave us financial security, we began to think of the other dreams we had hoped would be fulfilled. We had no children, and in those days fertility clinics were not prominent as in this age. The Korean war had been widely covered on television, and there was much concern about the many orphans that were uncared for in that country. Our earnings were now enough to keep a family, and we had a lovely house by the sea, so we started to make enquiries about the possibility of adopting Korean orphans. At that time we found this impossible because of all the red tape involved. The enquiries we made were through a Kircudbright council child worker. As a result of this we were contacted by the children's officer from Greenock, in those days a rather run down town near Glasgow. We were asked to take on three small children from their children's home. They were all under four years of age and were disturbed having been brought up by a single mother who herself had mental health problems. The children had been ill treated and were removed from the mother. It seemed a daunting job, but the children's officer pleaded with us to consider taking the children, for otherwise they would be left in a home. The disappointment of not being able to adopt Korean children was still fresh in our minds, and perhaps this was the way forward, although much consideration needed to be given to the idea. Adopting three children at once, all having special needs, was not what we had anticipated. We visited the children's home and met the children who were beautiful, although needing a lot of loving care. It was agreed that we should later have them for a two week visit in Kippford to see if the children could settle with us. The plan was for us to foster them, with the promise that we would be able to adopt them as soon as the court case was over. A bedroom for the boys was furnished with bunk beds, and we bought a cot for the baby. Other needful commodities were purchased ready for their visit. A date had been fixed, and as the time came near we were having difficulty making the final arrangements with the children's officer. Day after day, during the preceding week to their visit, I tried to contact the officer, and each time was fobbed off with some excuse. The day came and passed for their arrival and nothing happened. The children's officer never did contact us to apologise or explain what had happened. Later we discovered that the court case had gone in favour of the mother, and the children were returned to her. I can only think that the man was too cowardly to tell us the truth, after he had been so insistent that these three children could never return to their mother, and had pressed us so hard to have the children, assuring us that we would be able to adopt them.

Not long afterwards we were staying with a clergy family in Kinross as we overhauled their organ, and I told them this story. As a result of that visit we were put in touch with the church's adoption social worker, and about a year later we adopted our first baby, a little boy of Nigerian and Scottish parentage. Eighteen months later we adopted our second baby, a little girl, half Spanish and half Guianan. Both these children have given us much joy and we are so pleased that the Korean children and Greenock children did not materialise, for I know that our two children were especially meant for us. They are now grown up and I thank God for them, and will always be proud of them.

John's father took early retirement, and his parents moved up to live near us and bought a house in Dalbeattie. My father-in-law joined John and helped with the organ business. He had retired from management, but thoroughly enjoyed working with his hands building organs. John also employed a professional cabinet maker, and a young apprentice. John's mother was very happy living near to us again, and both parents were especially pleased that they now had two lovely grandchildren. Our order book began to fill up, and later we employed more people.

Our hope of working full time in the service of God had not been fulfilled, although building church pipe organs partly satisfied that dream. We still believed that one day we would serve God full time in the church. In the early days we thought that we would become missionaries, but this did not happen, and we continued with our lives knowing that when the time was right the door would open. One Sunday, the Primus of the Scottish Episcopal Church came to Dalbeattie, and the theme of his sermon was an appeal for someone to come forward into the full time ministry of the church. This was the door that we had been waiting to open. Our early Christian lives had been nurtured in a very fundamentalist church, but we found that the church where we were really happy and where we felt at home was the Episcopal Church in Scotland. The worship here was very fulfilling and we enjoyed the liturgy and fellowship, and it was here that we wanted to serve God.

The decision to go forward for ordination for full time ministry in the Anglican church was a joint decision, for it would affect both our lives. Once again we would be living frugally, having to account for each penny we spent. There were grants available to help with the fees for theological training, but after this initial two years of training we would be on a low stipend, especially during the curacy period. Even as rector the stipend would be a lot less than the money we had earned in business. However, tightening our belts was something with which we were already acquainted, although this time we had a family to care for. John went for various interviews, and it was decided that he would train in England, for there were no theological colleges in Scotland that catered for older men, and John was now reaching his thirty eighth birthday.

There would be little difficulty in selling our house, for it was in an ideal position, but the problem would be to sell the organ business as a going concern. A buyer was needed who would be willing, not only to buy the property, but also take over the order book, the tunings and the guarantees. The time scale, too, was tight as John had been offered a place at Worcester Theological College, and the term started in the autumn. The almost impossible happened and we managed to find a buyer. Our next problem was to find accommodation for the family in Worcester. All the properties in the Cathedral Close, used for ordinands, had been let, and it looked as if we would need to buy a house. This was not a good idea just for a two year period, but there seemed no other way. Another miracle happened, we received a letter from the diocesan chancellor. It seemed that his mother in law owned a large estate six miles out of Worcester, and one of her gardeners' houses was vacant, and she was willing for us to take up residency there.

Those two years had their high spots and low spots. John was away from the family from about six o'clock in the morning until eight o'clock at night, so he saw very little of our two children who were then fourteen months and three and a half years old. The bus service from the nearest village was infrequent so I was isolated. The gardener who lived next door to us, provided us with fresh fruit and vegetables, and we were blessed by living on a large, beautiful estate. There was a big lake in the grounds, and plenty of lovely places for me to walk with the children. The elderly lady who owned the estate, and lived in the mansion, took a great interest in our family, and was good with the children. What is more, she did not want any rent for the house.

We were well away from the sea, but the River Severn wound its way through Worcester, and we had bought a catamaran, which was moored at Diglis Basin. John had various free periods during college time, and it was not convenient for him to come home during these times, and would have been an added expense. He was able to walk down to the basin and work on the catamaran during his free time. The college holidays were long and we were able to enjoy them on the boat. That first summer holiday we motored down the River Severn and the ship canal, hoping to sail back up to Scotland. The day we intended to begin the journey north, dawned bright and clear. We tied up in the huge lock at Sharpness on our first stretch of the voyage. It was very nerve wracking, for although we were quite a reasonable size, a twenty six foot catamaran, we were dwarfed by all the boats sharing the lock. Among the vessels were small commercial ships, tugs and large expensive cruisers all crammed together. Our catamaran was very vulnerable. It took a long time for the motley collection of boats to be positioned and the level of water to be right for the lock gates to open. By the time this happened, the lovely, sunny, calm day had been transformed by a strong wind blowing up. When we came out of the lock the sea was rough and getting rougher. Our minds had to be made up quickly as to whether we should stay out to sea in wind which was building into a gale, or turn tail and come back into the lock before the gates were shut. The latter was chosen. We had learned much about the dangers of the sea on Heston, and were not prepared to take any risks with two small children aboard. While the spell of bad weather lasted, we motored back up the canal and moored there. Talking to the harbour master later, he assured us that we had chosen the right course, for even the larger vessels were being battered as they made their way down the estuary to the open sea. When the weather cleared we locked out again and sailed round the coast and ended up spending much of the holiday on the sands at Weston super Mare. The children enjoyed playing on the sands much more than being buffeted by the wind and sea on our way north.

Unfortunately, there was no suitable curate's house for us to spend the curacy years in Scotland, and it was quite a time before we returned to the country we had learned to love so much. Over the years we have served in a number of places, mainly in England, but John's last church was in the diocese of Galloway and Glasgow. Meanwhile the children have become adults and both succeeded in their chosen courses at university. They have both done extremely well, and I am very proud of them.

During this time I trained as a Lay Reader in the Church of England, and was able to help John in his ministry. The calling to full time ministry in the church was for both of us, but at that time it was not possible for women to be ordained. When women were allowed to train for ordination, at first just as deacons, I felt called by God to this ministry. Working in the church was a calling we had both received early in our lives, and it had taken many years before John's vocation was fulfilled, and even longer before it was possible for me to take the same route. I was accepted by the bishop, and my study course for the academic training for Non Stipendiary Ministry was a Bachelor of Divinity degree. My study was a course at London University as a distance learning student. Since I had not undertaken any formal education for a long time, except for the Reader Training, it was necessary to do a preliminary course first. Before attaining my degree John died of cancer. The exams for the degree were taken the year he died and an honours degree was achieved. During the year's interregnum I was able to work hard in the parish, which helped me cope with my grief. Unhappily, the new rector was unwilling to support my ordination, and after a year told me that there was an unwritten rule in the church that clergy widows do not remain in their husband's old parish. By this time I had been living in a flat for almost two years, in the nearby town of Kirkintilloch, which was part of the parish. It took a long time for me to sell the flat, but eventually it was sold and the move down south was made, to be nearer my children and elderly mother. John had come into the ministry late and died long before his retirement, so his pension was small, and my move was determined by house prices.

I had expected to be ordained in my new diocese since my training had been completed in Scotland with a B.D. honours degree, and the Bishop of Glasgow and Galloway had accepted me for ordination. This did not happen as the English dioceses have different rules, and my new diocese stipulated that the maximum age for ordination into the Non Stipendiary Ministry was sixty years, and I had turned sixty. This has been a great disappointment to me. Nevertheless, in the seven years I have been in England, I have continued to serve the church in many capacities, being relicensed as a Reader, and trained and licensed as a Diocesan Prayer Guide. I have also continued with my studies and in September I shall be awarded my Master of Theology degree in Oxford. The research for my dissertation was suggested by my tutor, on hearing about my disappointment concerning ordination. The dissertation was 'Ageism in the Church.' Life has not been easy, especially in these last few years, yet I know that I have the love and support of my family and friends, and above all a strong Christian faith which has enabled me to face the challenges of life.

Chapter 16   Reflections on my Spiritual Journey.

"I will meditate on all your work."   (Psalm 77 v. 12)

My dissertation for a Masters Degree was submitted last September, following three years of study. Since then some of my free time has been devoted to writing this book. It has been good looking back over my past life, and reliving some of the very poignant moments. I have been privileged to have enjoyed a varied life, with times of adventure and excitement, and times of ordinary routine chores. Throughout it all my Christian faith has been a firm foundation. During the various problems in life, comfort and reassurance has always rooted in my belief that there is a God who loves me. In this scientific, materialistic world, people need proof before believing in anything that they cannot touch or experience. Yet, many people realise the need of a spirituality within their lives, and are willing to turn to many out of the way cults and experiences, even resorting to drugs and alcohol to lift them out of the ordinary, often meaningless, world.

My time on Heston made me appreciate what a wonderful, beautiful world this is, in spite of the desecration and pollution the earth experiences at the hands of humanity. We often damage our earth by greed, power seeking and selfishness. Before starting work for the day, I spend an hour out in the countryside walking and treasuring the beauty of God's marvellous universe. My holidays, too, are very special times when I can venture farther afield and value the beauty of other parts of our country, or the different scenery of other lands. The many wonders of nature observed in those island years, the phosphorescence in the sea, the glory of the Northern Lights, and the many other marvels which we were privileged to share are no longer part of my life. Yet each morning as I walk, what ever the weather, nature speaks to me of God's love and provision.

A little while ago I was privileged to share in a sixteen day retreat in the north of Wales, where we spent the time learning how to help others find a satisfying spirituality. We had times of worship, quietness, activities, play, and great fellowship, and I enjoyed it all. The part I found most uplifting was setting out each morning to walk through the Welsh hills and lanes. I left the college about six o'clock in the morning, while the others slept, and had over an hour in solitude and oneness with nature. This is now the basis of my life. My life is busy as I work in many capacities in my church, but my strength and renewal come from these quiet times with God, revealed through nature. Both my children live at a distance, my daughter lives in Switzerland, and life can sometimes be lonely, yet it is also very fulfilling. My morning walk is a time of quiet reflection, a time of feeling at one with nature. Walking alone, whatever the weather, brings me close to God, gives me time to put problems into perspective, and to be thankful for the many blessings I have received in life.

This book began by reflecting on the future and the past on that first morning of the new millennium Revisiting the past has revived many memories of my physical journey on this earth. I want to end by sharing with you my spiritual reflections, some from the time spent in the distant past, but also with the insights given to me in the present time, and the more recent past. My early morning walks and the summer morning walks in North Wales, are a great encouragement, enabling me to put all the trials and uncertainties of life in perspective. Perhaps, my experiences may encourage others to look around and see God's presence in their every day situations of life, whatever the circumstances. Beauty, mystery, joy and a knowledge of belonging and peace, can be found in the world around us, wherever we find ourselves if we look for it. The sixteen day retreat was to explore ways of prayer and meditation. So often, our prayers are lists of petitions for ourselves and other people, interspersed with praise and thanksgiving. There is nothing wrong with this, but if prayer is a meeting with God and a conversation with him, then we must also listen as well as talk. We can hear God speaking to us in many ways, through reading, talking with others, music, art, and especially for me through nature. In the epitaph for Sir Christopher Wren in St. Paul's Cathedral, the words are written "If you are looking for his memorial, look around you." How true this is of God. We can find God by looking around his world, which is full of the excellence of his creation, but also speaks to us in symbols and parables, whether we are walking in the countryside, or aware of our surroundings in town or country.

The first morning's walk in Wales was one of exploration, for I had never stayed in this part of Wales before. This echoed the theme of the retreat, for we were exploring various ways of coming near to God. The college where the retreat was held was in a valley, and all walks led upwards towards the hills. Many of the lanes were flanked with banks topped with hedges of hazel, holly, briar and bramble. The narrow lanes were sheltered and intimate, reminiscent of my closeness to God. Now and again the hedge was interrupted by a field gate, and a whole new vista appeared of sun-dappled pastures grazed by sheep, with the hills rising steeply and topped with clouds. Prayers can be very personal, a closeness with God who intimately shares all our joys and sorrows, but they also open out into the world around us, and the larger view of the world is shared, revealing the joys, sorrows and needs of others. The hedges prevented the open view, yet served a useful purpose, protecting the sheep and cows, and preventing them from wandering and becoming lost. Our lives sometimes appear to be hedged in, and we long to break loose into the freedom beyond; yet the hedges of life are often there to protect us from going astray. Hedges hold us back from impetuousness, most of us are impatient and want to move on faster than is good for us. We need to learn the lessons necessary for the journey. In the Jewish Talmud, the rabbis talk of the Law of God being a hedge around the people to keep them safe. The hedges along the lane were fragrant with wild flowers, with some early fruit appearing. Birds had built their nests in the hedge, reminding us of new life, the fledglings having fled the nest long since. I find it useful to reflect on all the good thing concerning hedges, when I am impatient of restrictions and wanting to move on.

Hill walking is tiring, and I needed to rest now and again, to get my breath back, and this enabled me to look back over the way I had come. Life is often a struggle, and it is helpful to take time out to rest and look back, remembering the good things, and the way that we have been brought through past difficult times. The great joy on that first walk, was coming out from the shaded lane into the open sunlight. A hill rose up from the road circling the valley, and I climbed over the gate and struggled up to the top of the hill to enjoy a peaceful time looking down into the valley. Conquering the hill gave me a sense of achievement, reminding me of the steep hills of life, which when conquered give satisfaction and fulfilment. Each battle won in life gives us encouragement and the strength to press on with our lives, aiming at a new goal. It was not possible to stay at the top of the hill for long, for I needed to climb down and return to the college ready for the work of the day. Our spiritual lives have their heights and their depths. Some Christians seem to want to remain up in the heights, chasing after spiritual experiences to bring them personal fulfilment that pushes away the humdrum work. In the Gospel story which tells us about Jesus being transfigured and shining with glory, he talked with Moses and Elijah, and the disciples were filled with awe and wanted to build tents to stay there. The vision ended and they came down from the mountain for there was work to be done. The highlights of life give us strength and encouragement to come down and continue the work each of us has been given to accomplish.

The hill was bathed with the early morning sunlight, and it was good walking towards the sun, all shadows falling behind me. Ignatius, who was the founder of the Jesuits, wrote his exercises to help people on their spiritual journey. He refers to the good times in life as times of consolation, a word from the Latin meaning 'with the sun'. Times of desolation are times of walking away from the sun, times when it is unwise to make great decisions in life, for our mood is sombre and lacking the light so necessary for life. The whole of that walk illuminated my spiritual life, talking to me of my great need to embrace the 'Light of the World', Jesus, who is able to bring us through all struggles, disasters and disappointments. Walking gives me a sense of peace within, even when the physical world is noisy. Our lives, however much buffeted and battered by our circumstances, can be stilled by an inward peace, like the still centre of a hurricane.

During my walks on Gentleshaw Common and on Cannock Chase it is good to enjoy the early morning quietness. Often I meet no one, but sometimes there are people who are out early exercising their dogs. The part of the Chase nearest to me is wooded, a mixture of deciduous trees and conifers. The conifers seem to have shallow roots, and I sometimes come across a tree that has been uprooted by a gale. The oaks and ashes have deep roots which anchor them and keep them safe through most storms. Our Christian lives need to be deeply rooted in faith. It is those who have strong roots, who weather the storms of life. People with a shallow faith, sometimes appearing to be strong and out going Christians, fall at the first hurdle in their spiritual lives, having no depths to draw on. Their lives outwardly appear to be solid and steadfast, like the trees before the storms and gales hit them. The large canopy of leaves catch the wind, and if the roots are shallow, this expedites the trees downfall. Just as a tree draws its nutrients and water from the soil through its roots, so we grow in faith and strength as we draw deeply on the water of life, God's indwelling Spirit.

As on that first morning of the millennium, mist can blanket out the scenery. It can be cold and dreary, like the depression that can descend over our lives when life seems shrouded with problems, and the future appears bleak and sombre. One of the Welsh misty mornings was exciting, for as I walked, shapes of trees emerged from the mist, and after a while a pale, creamy-lemon sun became visible, heralding the dispersal of the white haze. That morning the sun broke through and was a symbol of God's light and love breaking through into our lives and dispelling the doubt and gloom. Sometimes the fog and mist is dispersed by the wind rising. The Hebrew word for wind is the same word that the Bible uses for spirit, and reminds me that although Jesus is no longer on earth to heal and comfort, the Holy Spirit is with us to guide and lead us, and to disperse the uncertainties in our lives, whatever our state of mind or circumstances. Once the mist had cleared the pale sunlight bathed the countryside and high lighted all the beauty surrounding me. Even the grasses along the edge of the lane sparkled like jewels as the droplets of water from the mist reflected the sunlight. The early beginnings of my spiritual journey as a Christian had very restricted ideas about God and about people. As the years have passed I have moved on and my views and beliefs have widened. The many beautiful colours that are emitted when light is reflected, whether from a diamond, or droplets of water, show me that our spirituality is a reflection of God. Just as we see different colours in the prism as our viewing position alters, so we as people can appreciate the different gifts and beliefs of others, which are just as sincere as ours. We too, reflect different aspects of faith and love, but all reflect from the same source.

In Britain the weather is often the topic of conversation. At the time that I am writing this, the weather is a great issue, for we are half way through July and have had very little summer weather up until now. We moan about the rain, yet it is the rain that makes our country so green and fruitful, that fills the rivers and lakes which give us so much pleasure. When my husband was alive our favourite holiday destination was Israel. We valued experiencing the joy of seeing and walking in the land where Jesus lived and died for us. One year we were told that they had had a very good winter. By this they meant that there had been more rain than usual, and the sea of Galilee and the River Jordan were well filled. In countries where there is little rainfall, its value is appreciated much more. Without the rain life cannot survive. Just as the rain is necessary to life for growth, so also is the sun. The life giving sun in nature not only gives warmth and light, but provides the energy for plants to combine the elements they need to produce food, which is necessary for all life. These attributes of nature are so symbolic of our spiritual lives. Without the warmth and love of the light of the world, Jesus, and the living water, the Holy Spirit, our spiritual lives will not only cease to grow, but will wither and die. I like the passage from Isaiah chapter 35, which tells about the Lord coming to save his people. It speaks of streams in the desert and springs of water welling up from the thirsty ground. One of my favourite places in Israel is Caesarea Philippi. This was the place where Peter was inspired to declare that Jesus was the Messiah, the one sent by God. Here springs of water bubble up from the ground and run together to form streams. These small streams join and tumble over the rocks and form one of the tributaries of the River Jordan. This is the river that is the main water source in Israel, and is used to irrigate the land, and is the means of bringing forth abundant crops to sustain the people. As Christians filled with God's Spirit, we too have his joy and life giving presence bubbling up in us, and together we can work in unity and become a river, bringing spiritual life and joy to all those around in barren places.

While I was staying in Wales we had a period of very hot nights, and it was difficult to sleep because of the heat. One morning, after a poor night's sleep, I was tired and tempted to give up the struggle of climbing to the top of the hilly lane, and instead take a shortcut, which would lead me down hill and back to the college. The temptation was resisted and I continued on my upward track and was fully rewarded by the views of an undiscovered part of the region. The satisfaction and joy of finding new places would have been missed, had I succumbed to the temptation of a quick and easy route back. That walk was a picture of life's temptations, and how we miss so much when we take the easy way out. During hot weather, with little rain, the streams and pools become dried up, and a good storm and down pour of rain is needed to revitalise the countryside, and rush down the stream beds, clearing away the rubbish and refilling the pools and lakes. We have dry times in our lives, when everything seems to be too much trouble, and apathy sets in. We too, need to be stirred up, and all the hindrances and blockages in our lives flushed out and replaced with life giving water.

Wherever I walk, there is always wild life to be seen. On the Chase we are lucky to have red deer, and other species, roaming the woods and moors. The common, where I most often walk these days, does not boast the more exotic animals, but there are rabbits and squirrels to be seen and many birds. The black birds, robins, wrens and many other birds that visit my garden give me much pleasure. The sparrows twitter and quarrel amongst themselves, and Jesus said that God cares even for the sparrows, so how much more will he care for us. I miss watching all the sea birds that were so abundant and diverse on Heston, and all the creatures to be seen in the sea and on the large stretches of mud flats as the tide goes out. The waders follow the receding tide, searching the mud for the small animals left high and dry, the curlews probe the mud with their curved beaks. Jelly fish lie exposed and drying on the rack and sands, along with seaweed and discarded rubbish that sometimes reached our shores. Yet soon the tide comes flooding in, washing away the detritus and cleansing the sands, bringing nutrients and renewed life to mussels and other shell fish clinging to the rocks. Like the tide, God's love comes flooding into our lives, cleansing, forgiving and renewing us.

Until 1979 I had very good health, and had never had any serious illness or operation. Since then I have had many operations, including two radical mastectomies. In between the various operations for the removal of tumours, which have occurred every few years, I have been blessed with good health. In 1997 I had almost a month in hospital for a chest reconstruction, this was to remove all the chest tissue, as it was clear that throughout the past eighteen years the cancer cells had not been completely removed. At the time this radical operation was difficult and painful, but I believed that it was worth all the upheaval to remove all the cancer once and for all. For the following two years I felt healthier and better able to work than for many years. My church work as a Lay Minister, involves taking services, teaching and pastoral work. For several years I have had the privilege of taking funerals, and my bereavement work brought me into contact with many in the community who no longer come to church. During these years I have discovered that many people who do not attend church still have a strong faith, and a spiritual life.

After the radical operation I believed that my cancer had been cured, and I was happy to take on more work in the church and in the community. Work in the diocese was under taken, and also I became a school governor, regularly taking school assemblies. In the spring of 1999 a bone scan was taken to determine the treatment for an old knee injury. You can imagine my devastation when I was informed that the bone scan revealed that the cancer had spread into my bones. Various ways of dealing with the pain and strengthening the bones were discussed. When I protested that I felt healthier than I had been for many years, and that I had no pain, I was assured, that this treatment would be necessary as the disease advanced. This was unbelievable, yet the hospital staff were so sure that the cancer had spread. That night was spent being angry with the world and especially with God. Because I felt so well I really believed that I had been cured, and that is the reason I had taken on all this new work in the church and community. It now seemed that I would need to relinquish it all. By morning I was in no state or mood to go walking or have my usual Bible reading and time of meditation. In spite of this, an inner conviction pushed me to open my Bible and read the chapter for the day. At that time I was reading the Bible from cover to cover, something I had not done for half a century, and the book I was reading was boring and uninspiring. That morning when I eventually opened my Bible, I was surprised to find that the chapters of genealogies that I had been struggling through were ended. The chapter contained David's prayer for his son Solomon, who was the one chosen to build the Temple. The verse that jumped off the page as I read was *'Be strong and of good courage, and act. Do not be afraid or dismayed, for the Lord God, my God, is with you. He will not fail you or forsake you, until all the work for the service of the house of the Lord is finished.' (1 Chronicles ch. 28 v 20.)*

After this affirmation of God's presence and love for me I felt confident that I was healed and would complete all the work that the Lord has given me to do. I did, however, feel very guilty about my lack of trust and shouting at God that night when the various members of the medical profession were so certain that I had bone cancer. Shortly after that time one of the Lichfield Diocesan 'Schools of Prayer' was held. My involvement in these Diocesan days and 'Schools of Prayer' in the parishes, was part of the new work with which I had become involved. The plenary talk for the day was by the Very Revd. Gordon Mursell, Provost of the Cathedral in Birmingham. During his inspiring talk he emphasised how much God appreciated our honesty in prayer. He wanted us to pour out our grief and anger, like the Psalmists of old, preferring this to our boring, sometimes unfeeling lists of requests. This cheered me and lessened my feeling of guilt. Because I believed strongly that cancer had not spread into my bones, the onchologist agreed to wait for six months before starting new therapy. At the end of this period I was still well and without pain, and he agreed that I might be right, and after a lapse of another six months the bone scans were repeated. That visit was in the spring and the the 'hot spots' had disappeared from my pelvis and lower spine, although there was one in the lumbar region. Cancer does not jump, but spreads, therefore the bone scan had not shown a spread of cancer, but some bone degeneration, which is often found in people of my age. My work in school and the diocese has continued, along side all my church work. Those words of hope and encouragement from the Bible were given to me, and thankfully later proved to be true.

We all travel life's journey, and have a story to tell about childhood and family life, joys and hardships. All of us too, can have a spiritual journey, and this does not depend upon the vicissitudes of our physical existence. Many people travel through life knowing that something is missing, and strive to fill the void with things that do not satisfy. My prayer is that all of you will find hope, love and satisfaction in your lives. Augustine, who lived in the fourth century, wisely wrote that we all have a spiritual need and cannot rest until we find that need in God. Not all of my dreams have been fulfilled, but I continue to travel both on my physical and spiritual journeys, having hope and an inward peace and a knowledge of God's love for me, a love and peace that is offered to everyone. (60722)